Why Don't Lions Chase Mice?

An Introduction to Energy-Based Economics

Tim Watkins

WHY DON'T LIONS CHASE MICE?

AN INTRODUCTION TO ENERGY-BASED ECONOMICS

© TIM WATKINS 2020

ISBN: 9798674725398

All rights reserved. No part of this publication may be reproduced, stored in a retrieval system, or transmitted, in any form or by any means, electronic, mechanical, photocopying, recording or otherwise, without the prior permission of the copyright owner.

WAYE FORWARD LTD
WWW.WAYEFORWARD.COM

Contents

Why don't lions chase mice?	1
Adam's curse	9
Energy and value: the basics	19
The other tendency for the rate of profit to fall	27
Productivity	35
A brief alternative history of the industrial age	43
Getting the economy wrong	75
Complexity and the myth of sustainability	103
The limits to fossil fuels	111
Energy, resources, population and consumption	117
Where next?	125
A brown new deal	131

WHY DON'T LIONS CHASE MICE?

No, it is not a trick question. Indeed, the answer you gave is probably the correct one. A lion is a very large and powerful animal whereas a mouse is a very small but surprisingly nimble creature. Unless a mouse were foolish enough to walk into a lion's mouth or at least stand beneath its paw, it is doubtful, that a lion – which spends around 18 hours a day resting and sleeping – could be sufficiently roused to attempt the chase.

This is easy enough to understand, but beneath this superficial answer is a piece of physics which is profoundly important to explaining almost every aspect of our way of life. A simple or small calorie is the amount of energy required to raise the temperature of a gram of water (at normal atmospheric pressure) by one degree centigrade. A Kcal (i.e. a thousand calories) – the measure of energy that we typically call a calorie when applied to food – is thus the amount of energy required to heat a kilogram of water by a degree. The average human in a developed economy requires between 2,000 and 3,000 Kcals per day (although, sadly, we tend to consume many more). A lion requires some 8-9,000 Kcals per day. And unlike humans who have access to high-calorie starchy foods, lions must get their calories from animal protein (muscle) and fat. A reasonably well-fed mouse contains around 30 Kcals; and so a lion would have to catch and consume more than 280 mice a day to sustain itself. While not entirely impossible in ideal conditions, in ordinary circumstances the lion would find itself burning more calories chasing the mice than it would receive in return.

A small domestic cat – itself a far nimbler creature than a lion – might fare better on a diet of mice. But lions are better off working in teams to kill large prey such as water buffalo which contain up to 500,000 Kcals; more than enough to share around a pride and have left overs for scavengers like hyenas and vultures.

Only plants have the luxury of obtaining the energy to maintain and grow themselves directly from sunlight. Every other living being must first *expend* energy in order to obtain energy:

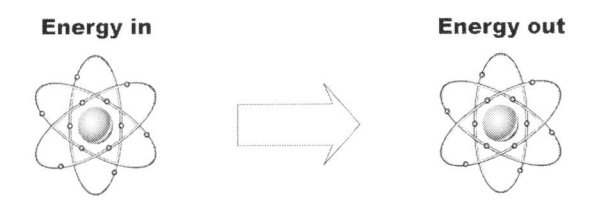

Energy in ⟹ **Energy out**

This is expressed in several (more or less synonymous) ways:

- EROEI – Energy Return on Energy Invested
- EROI – Energy Return on Investment
- ECoE – Energy Cost of Energy

Each is a measure of the value of an activity. An energy return of 1:1 is not normally[†] worth the expenditure. Expending more energy than is obtained is positively life-threatening:

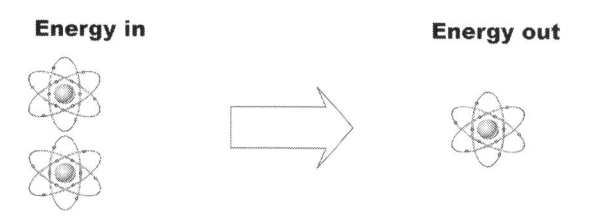

Energy in → **Energy out**

Just gaining *some* additional energy may not be sufficient either:

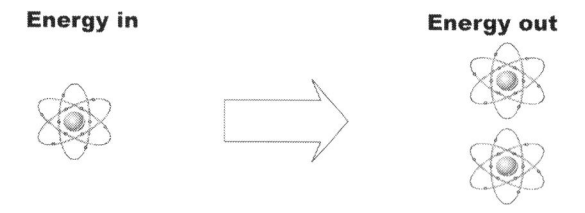

Energy in → **Energy out**

Remember how modern humans need between 2,000 and 3,500 Kcals per day? Only a half or less of this can be devoted to the jobs we do to get the currency with which to buy life's essentials. Around 1,000 Kcals is required just to allow a human body to continue existing in a healthy condition. And some Kcals at least have to be expended on various non-work activities (including procreating the species). It might be that a minimum EROI of 4:1 is needed just to sustain human life:

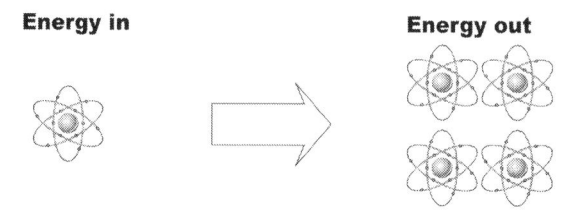

Energy in → **Energy out**

[†] There are circumstances in a modern industrial economy where a negative EROI might be of limited use. For example, coal-rich but oil poor states such as inter-war Germany may opt to use more coal-based energy than they obtain in the form of oil-based energy.

In addition to this limitation on our energy needs, we must also come to terms with the laws of thermodynamics. In particular, the second law of thermodynamics is that when energy is converted from one form to another, a proportion of that energy is *always* lost as waste heat. When we work or exercise, our bodies heat up and we have to produce sweat in order to evaporate the heat into the surrounding atmosphere. The same used to happen when our ancestors hunted animals or worked the fields to grow crops:

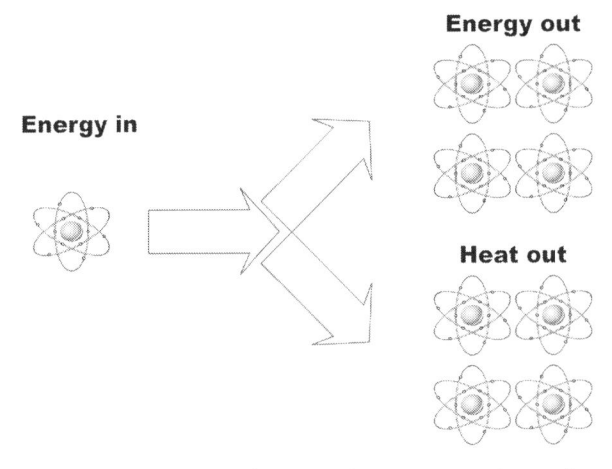

Energy in → **Energy out** / **Heat out**

Accounting for the additional energy lost as waste heat, the minimum EROI needed to sustain human life might be 8:1 or more; depending upon how *efficiently* we are able to use the energy available to us.

For most of the 250,000 years or so that humans have been around, our calorie intake has come from the direct sunlight that fed the plants at the base of the food chain. We may have supplemented that energy with renewables like wind and water power – which are also a product of sunlight – but the annual growth of plants provided a hard limit upon the energy we could utilise. What makes the modern world different is that we broke into planet Earth's massive store of fossilised sunlight; coal, oil and gas. For the first time in history, humans were able to escape the vagaries of the seasons. The modern economy is more complex, but we could not escape the limitations of EROI and thermodynamics.

Fossil fuels provide vastly more energy than the starches and sugars in the foods we eat. A kilogram of coal, for example, contains around 6,000 Kcals – enough to sustain 2-3 humans if only we could consume

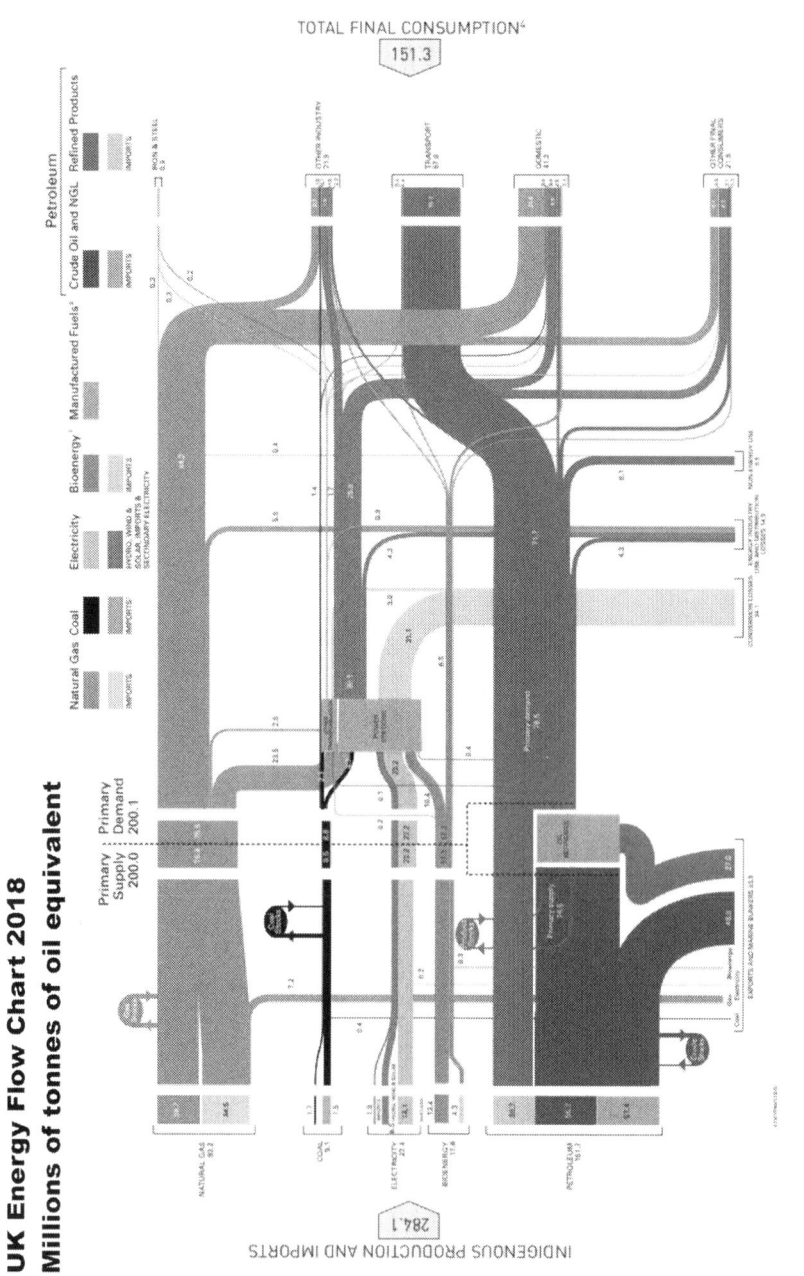

UK Energy Flow Chart 2018
Millions of tonnes of oil equivalent

https://assets.publishing.service.gov.uk/government/uploads/system/uploads/attachment_data/file/818151/Energy_Flow_Chart_2018.pdf

it directly. Mining that coal, however, requires that we expend energy up front. And so coal – along with any other fuel source – has an EROI of its own. Here, however, we encounter a problem seldom encountered by lions; or mice and men for that matter. Not all coal is equal. There is a massive difference, for example, in the coal seams which used to jut out of the sides of Welsh hills prior to the industrial revolution and the fractured and tortured seams which remain thousands of feet beneath the floors of today's Welsh valleys – too difficult and too expensive to ever be recovered. The difference is that the EROI of fossil fuels tends to decline because humans extract the easiest deposits first.

When the EROI of coal dropped precipitously around the beginning of the twentieth century it had catastrophic consequences. The leading political world powers of the day – Germany, Great Britain and France – were each built around coal-powered economies. But as the EROI of the coal they consumed fell, so too did the rate of growth across their economies. And while this is not a sufficient explanation for the outbreak of war in August 1914, it is an often overlooked factor which generated greater competition and more intense rivalries.

The one saving grace was that by 1914 a superior fossil fuel – oil – was beginning to make its presence felt. In addition to having a higher energy-density, the fuels derived from oil came in liquid form and so could be easily stored and transported. As a consequence, many of the industrial processes which had been powered by coal were switched to oil; leaving the remaining coal to power the remaining – largely heavy – industrial processes like steel manufacture and railways.

In switching from coal to oil, we massively increased EROI across the economy. That is, there was far more energy left over after we had subtracted the energy required to extract more energy, to allow a massive expansion of non-energy economic activity. Nevertheless, by the end of the twentieth century we were experiencing the same "EROI crunch" that had occurred with coal a century earlier. All of the cheap and easy oil fields were depleting, and the smaller and more expensive deposits that we were replacing them with provided less energy return on the energy invested.

To return to lions and mice, we find ourselves in a situation in which plant growth has failed and the animals we might normally eat have died from starvation. We wouldn't normally eat mice, but now we will attempt to catch any animal that we can, even one as small as a mouse.

But while this might keep us alive for a little longer, only if we can find larger prey will we be able to guarantee the survival of our species.

In the modern world, it is less the species than the complex globalised life support systems which we developed back in the days when energy was plentiful which is at risk. In those days, manufacturing goods and growing food on the opposite side of the planet from where they are consumed seemed to make sense because the cost of transporting them using *cheap* oil-powered ships and aeroplanes was so low. Now, as the EROI of oil itself falls, it is only a matter of time before the most energy-consuming goods and foods must either be re-localised or simply abandoned altogether. Other activities, too, will become increasingly strained. The morning commute – not just from suburbs into city centres, but from city to city – which became a normal feature of daily life in the late twentieth century is already decreasing. More and more people find that the cost of running a vehicle or using public transport is so expensive that they are better off taking a local job that pays less.

The question – which nobody has managed to resolve definitively – is what is the minimum EROI required to maintain a modern economy? Some aspects of modern life, such as a basic secondary education, can be maintained at a relatively low EROI whereas the arts and more specialist forms of medicine require a much higher EROI to continue:

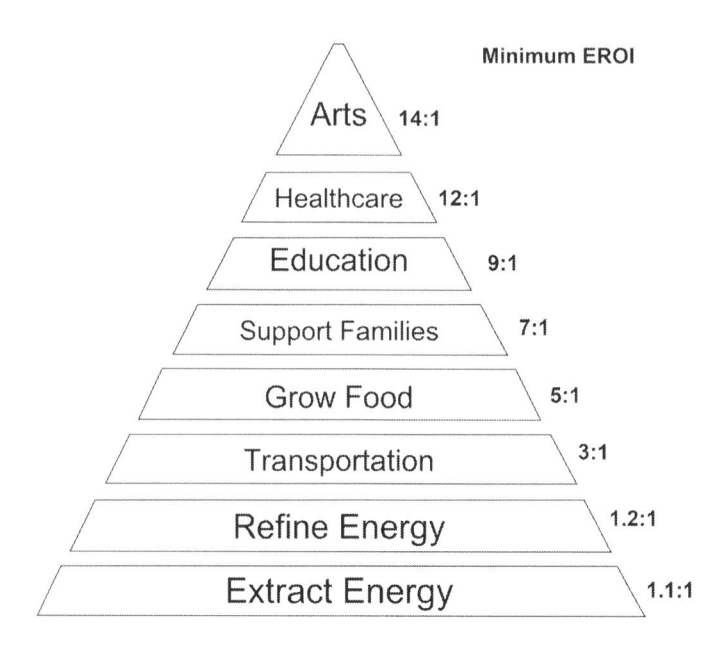

Minimum EROI

- Arts — 14:1
- Healthcare — 12:1
- Education — 9:1
- Support Families — 7:1
- Grow Food — 5:1
- Transportation — 3:1
- Refine Energy — 1.2:1
- Extract Energy — 1.1:1

Unfortunately, there is little agreement over what exactly our combined EROI for energy from all sources actually is. The remaining conventional oil remains above 20:1 whereas light oil from fracking comes in at around 5:1. Oil from bitumen sands is around 2.5:1 and corn ethanol (biofuel) is energy negative. Industrial scale wind turbines have an EROI of 20:1, but only if we overlook the fossil fuels which have to be added to provide a reliable flow of energy and to maintain them over the course of their lifespan – the energy might be renewable; the technology most certainly isn't. Nuclear from pressurised water reactors is around 15:1, while solar farms come in at around 5:1.

Prior to the Covid-19 pandemic at least, climate change was widely held as the crisis of our age. With the energy available to the economy already declining prior to SARS-CoV-2 embarking upon its world tour, however, a near-term energy crunch may prove far more deadly. That few people have even been aware of a looming energy problem is in large part because humans have never had to pay the full cost of the benefits we have derived from fossil fuels. For most people – including economists who ought to know better – energy is just another relatively cheap economic input. And since for the best part of three centuries we have enjoyed growing energy return on energy invested, most people take for granted that "clever people somewhere else" will come up with some other form of energy with which to unleash another round of economic growth.

At the time of writing, though, such alternative energy only exists in theory or in costly and unsustainable laboratory experiments. At the commercial/industrial scale, the only energy sources currently available to us *necessitate* a shrinking of the economy at a rate even worse than the self-inflicted economic shutdown in response to the pandemic.

Energy is the life-force behind *all* human activity. As contrarian economist Steve Keen puts it, "Capital without energy is a statue; labour without energy is a corpse." As the remainder of this book explains, the reason we should all care about why lions don't chase mice is because it is the same reason why advanced globalised economies *must* collapse if the quantity of energy upon which they were built is no longer available. At stake is almost everything that we take for granted about our modern way of life.

As we shall see, the choice ahead of us is stark. We are not facing the kind of crisis which can be solved with a different economic theory, a change of political party in government or even a new system of government. The laws we must grapple with are not like man (and woman)-made social distancing or road speed laws. They are the physical boundaries of the universe itself. It matters not one jot whether the red team or the blue team is in office when EROI drops below the ratio required to maintain industrial civilisation. The only question left for us to resolve are:

- Can we do anything to *increase* EROI, and if not,
- What is the least damaging way to *de-grow* an economy?

By the end of this book, I hope to convince readers that there is still a window – albeit a rapidly closing one – of opportunity to achieve one or other of these outcomes. However, I would caution that so long as humanity continues to be preoccupied with greed, personal gain and the relative trivialities of the 24 hour news cycle, then we will hand the process of de-growth to Mother Nature; and we most certainly will not enjoy the outcome.

Adam's Curse

There is something unique about human beings which separates us from every other lifeform on the planet. But the key difference is so obvious that almost all are blind to it. In Chapter seven of Volume One of *Das Kapital*, Karl Marx sets out the common understanding of the difference:

> *"A spider conducts operations that resemble those of a weaver, and a bee puts to shame many an architect in the construction of her cells. But what distinguishes the worst architect from the best of bees is this, that the architect raises his structure in imagination before he erects it in reality."*

This conscious ability to create artefacts from the primary materials of the planet – which begins with flint axes and leads to steam trains, radio sets, rockets to the moon, supersonic airliners, mobile phones and metropolitan cities – certainly *appears* to put humans into a class of their own. Elsewhere however, Marx qualifies this, observing that there is "a germ" of this ability in other species. Today we can observe tool use in several ape and avian species. It is also clear that apes, birds and pigs display embryonic cognitive abilities similar to our own. Evidence that these creatures *learn* this behaviour is seen in studies of their interaction with humans. For example, herons have been observed copying anglers and using insects and bread as bait to lure fish. Several bird species place nuts on roads, where passing vehicles will crack the shells open.

Consciously acting upon the world is not, then, the thing that distinguishes humans from animals... at least, not entirely. Rather than looking to Marx for an answer, we could do a lot worse than to turn to that old English imperialist Rudyard Kipling. In *The Jungle Book*, he sets out one of the two things that makes humanity unique:

> *"By Red Flower Bagheera meant fire, only no creature in the jungle will call fire by its proper name. Every beast lives in deadly fear of it, and invents a hundred ways of describing it."*

Fire predates humanity. Sometime in our ancestral past, a hominid ape from which we are all descended overcame the inherent fear of fire and began to control it. In doing so – to borrow a modern managerial phrase – it outsourced an important fraction of its digestive system. Where other creatures had to spend hours chewing and then digesting the food they needed, our hominid ape ancestors let fire do the job. The result – over millennia – was the evolution of smaller teeth, weaker jaws and shorter digestive tracts. Less obviously, the energy saved provided our ancestors with the time to think about and interact with the world around them. Where every other creature was at the mercy of the passing seasons, our ancestors began to shape the landscape around them to mitigate, at least to some degree, these changes.

We know that modern humans originated in Africa, because it is the only continent on Earth where a large number of large mammal species can still be found. Evolving alongside the humans, these animals learned just how dangerous humans were, and learned to give them a wide birth. The large mammal species on other continents were less fortunate. Fire – and the host of technologies (stone and bone tools, spears, bows and arrows, skin clothing, pottery, etc. – provided the means for humans to range beyond the warm equatorial regions of Africa.

In this way, we added our own curse to that of Adam. Clothing – itself a product of the technologies we produced with the time afforded to us by outsourcing part of our digestive system – allowed humans to migrate north and south of the hot zones where our species originated. Human remains have, for example, been found in caves across Europe; a region that would have been uninhabitable in winter without fire and clothing.

It is here, too, that we find the other thing which separates humans from the other life on Earth; and, again, it is a form of outsourcing. Cave paintings and score marks are the first efforts to outsource memory – leaving a record of past experience which other humans can learn from without having to directly experience the same thing. The more we outsourced energy, the more time we freed up to develop our attempts at recording our experience of the world, until our ancestors developed early alphabets and number systems which might be recorded on sticks, stones, clay tablets and early forms of paper.

As with technologies for harnessing energy, once the basics of reading, writing and arithmetic had been developed, specialist scribes could be employed; initially to write and later to publish our external memory. From the printing press to photography and the World Wide Web, increases in the energy available to us have allowed us to massively expand our collective external memory. And as our collective memory has expanded, so our societies and civilisations have – for better or worse – expanded to take over the entire planet.

As they spread out across Europe, Asia and across the land bridge to the Americas, our ancestors left a trail of devastation in their wake (including – possibly – the first genocide, when our branch of humans wiped out the Neanderthals). The archaeological records show that when humans first arrived in a region they made large spear and arrow heads for killing big prey. But over the centuries these artefacts shrink in size until they end up being no bigger than what is required for hunting rabbits and rats. Humans have always spelled extinction for other wildlife unfortunate enough to encounter us. But prior to the modern industrial age there were never enough of us to bring about a mass extinction. Our cave-dwelling ancestors had a relatively limited impact upon their environment.

There are, though, only so many caves to go around. And the local food supply can only last for so long in the face of an assault from creatures with external memories and energy-harnessing/saving technologies. So in time our ancestors brought down yet another curse upon our heads; *artificial* shelter. Building structures against the worst of the elements allowed people to move into previously uninhabited regions. Some shelters were temporary and could be packed away and moved as the people traversed the landscape following the food. But more permanent structures began to arise in regions where people learned to cultivate plants and domesticate animals. This permanence ushered in a new and revolutionary stage in human development.

Bands of humans in warm, fertile regions such as the Nile Valley, the Euphrates-Tigris plain, the Indus Valley and along the Yellow River began to cultivate crops as a more efficient survival strategy to hunting and gathering. The advantages were less clear-cut than you might think. In terms of *individual* health, the switch to agriculture was negative. Reliance upon starchy grass crops rotted teeth, stunted growth and shortened life expectancy. For society as a whole, however, agriculture provided massive returns. Stratification and specialisation began to emerge in the early agrarian economies as new classes of urban dwellers were able to survive on the surplus food produced by the agricultural labourers. This led to the development of the first civilisations – urban societies that *had* to import food and goods in order to survive and grow. The relative egalitarian arrangements in hunter-gatherer bands were replaced by hierarchical social structures ruled over by Kings, Queens, Emperors and Empresses and guarded by the first organised military forces.

Fire continued to provide the external energy basis even for these new civilisations. Fire powered the forges and ovens which allowed the civilisation to maintain itself and the people to feed themselves. The complexity of the early civilisations, however, began to obscure the importance of fire, as the new technologies and specialisations of the new agrarian age *appeared* to be more important. Other sources of external energy became important too. Work animals were bred to carry out the most arduous agricultural tasks. Tidal dams, water wheels and windmills provided humans with the means to concentrate diffuse solar energy. Sails sped and extended the range of sea transport.

Agriculture provided a hedge against the kind of collapse that hunter-gatherers regularly experienced when climatic changes and over-consumption impacted the foods they depended upon. But agriculture was never a *guarantee* of survival. Indeed, some of the practices that were central to early agriculture – such as irrigation and deforestation – served to undermine the land base in the longer-term. One of the earliest crimes against humanity was the practice of salting a neighbouring society's land. Too much salt in the soil causes crops to fail, and famine ensues. But early agrarian societies did not need an external enemy to salt their fields – irrigation gradually did the same thing. And so lands that were once the most fertile on the planet gradually died; sped on their way by deforestation which exposed the topsoil to the elements. As Derrick Jensen says,[1] "forests precede us and deserts dog our heels."

The problem was that civilisations that had grown up when food production was at its height faced major problems as the food supply declined. Expanding into new areas might offset this, so too might pillaging neighbouring peoples. But once the food supply began to collapse, one way or another, the civilisation's attempt to sustain itself at its existing complexity, population and standard of living doomed it to collapse.

In this process, civilisations do not simply retreat to the conditions that prevailed the last time the food supply was this small, even if this was only a few decades before. Instead, they tend to unravel completely; ushering in a dark age from which a new – and usually less complex – civilisation must begin again.

Our tendency is to view the process of the rise and fall of civilisation in technological terms. In the British Isles, for example, people lived for millennia in primitive Stone, Bronze and Iron Age settlements at a very low level of technology. The arrival of the Romans marked the start of a massive technological revolution, the scars of which can still be found throughout the landscape. The remains of Roman buildings are still regularly discovered, complete with discarded Roman artefacts, across Britain. This is in stark contrast to the scant remains of earlier Iron Age settlements and, indeed, of the Anglo Saxon settlements that grew up in the centuries after the Romans had left. It is only with the arrival of the Normans from the eleventh century that we begin to find enduring settlements based around older Roman technologies.

Technology, however, is a product of *energy*. When food was the only energy available to our earliest ancestors, a few rudimentary tools were all that they had. Fire allowed more activity, which in turn allowed the development and improvement of a much wider range of technology. Agriculture, animal power and the harnessing of wind and water power allows for an even greater range of technology. Take away the fire, the food, the water and the wind, however, and people are rapidly plunged into a far less technological state.

In the Bible, Adam's (and Eve's) curse† – the punishment for eating the forbidden fruit – was that men from then on would be forced to labour in the field (and that women would experience pain in childbirth). This, though, is only half of the curse. The real hardship is that *even* just to labour in the fields requires that we maintain those other external energy sources and energy-saving tools, clothes and shelters without which an agrarian economy could not operate. We must not only constantly replace the food that we depend upon; we must reproduce the fuel for the fire, the work animals and the machinery by which we harness the power of the tide and the wind. We must continually maintain and replace the tools, clothing and the shelters. And, of course, we must reproduce ourselves.

Therein is yet another curse. Like every other creature on the planet, we attempt to hedge against the natural attrition of our species. Beyond (in space and time) the affluent regions of the modern world, couples generally produce more than two offspring as a hedge against death in childbirth, childhood diseases, accidental deaths, etc. In periods of

---
† Eve suffered a lot worse. The snake, though, got off lightly, being cursed only to crawl around on its belly for the rest of its days... something that snakes are pretty well adapted to do anyway.

benign climate and good harvests, populations could grow accordingly. This, in turn allowed the economy itself to grow, creating even more abundance. The problem was (and is) that our population – like our civilisation – was (and is) vulnerable to collapse in the event that the larger population could not be supported.

Trade is an important means of mitigating this problem. A simple, enclosed economy would have to produce all of its food – and the goods to support food production – internally. A more efficient alternative is to specialise in the production of a smaller range of foods and goods best suited to local conditions; and then to trade these with neighbouring societies in exchange for foods and goods which cannot be produced locally. This is how the world's first "global" economy – the interconnected empires and kingdoms of the Bronze Age Eastern Mediterranean – functioned. Tin and copper were imported from as far afield as Cornwall to the north and Afghanistan to the east. Meanwhile, trade ships criss-crossed the Mediterranean carrying goods from each of the trading civilisations.

For a long time, archaeologists believed that this interconnected network of trading civilisations was destroyed by external invaders – the "sea peoples" documented in some of the artefacts of the period. More recently, though, new evidence suggests that the collapse was longer and slower, and was the result of a series of interconnected crises which gradually sapped the resilience of the civilisations. A shift to a cooler climate resulted in less rainfall, and so smaller harvests. Seismic events in the region caused earthquakes and tsunamis which destroyed whole towns. Civilisations began hoarding their locally produced foods and goods, causing trade routes to falter and laying the conditions for war. The arrival of the sea peoples – probably migrants fleeing similar catastrophes on the islands of Sicily and Sardinia – was merely the last in a long line of crises which mortally undermined the Bronze Age Mediterranean economy.

In the period since, empires have risen and fallen time and again. The broad sweep of rise and fall is much the same:

- Improved climatic conditions generate abundant food
- Abundant food allows population growth
- Larger populations generate surplus food
- Surplus food frees up a portion of the population to specialise in non-food activities

- A portion of the specialist population develops and refines the food growing technologies
- Improved technologies allow even more food surplus, an even larger population and even more specialisation
- Eventually the system *overshoots* its food and resource base
- The higher population can only be sustained by further exploiting domestic producers and/or conquering or pillaging neighbouring peoples
- Eventually even exploitation and pillage runs out of steam as no further *economically useful*[†] peoples can be pillaged (either because the neighbour is too backward to be worth pillaging or because the neighbour is too powerful to risk the attempt)
- Further collapse ensues as governmental specialisations (government, administration, military) begin to break down; trade within the civilisation ceases as regions and localities hoard food and goods; corruption runs rife; those at the base of the civilisation eventually walk away
- The peoples left on the land once encompassed by the civilisation revert to earlier and less complex economic arrangements from where, next time the climate is favourable, a new civilisation may rise from the ashes.

Modern civilisation is different; but not in the way most people imagine. The prevailing orthodoxy holds that today's truly globalised civilisation is the culmination of a broad sweep of *progress* which begins with the philosophers of ancient Greece as revived during the intellectual revolution of the European Enlightenment and propelled into the stratosphere by the scientific and technological revolution that both created and grew from the Industrial Revolution. Whereas only a tiny percentage of the population of the earliest agricultural civilisations could be spared from the fields to specialise in state or artisan activities, in modern western states less than 2 percent of the population work the land; the other 98 percent of us have been *apparently* liberated from Adam's curse by the wonders of technologies such as tractors, combine harvesters and even satellite controlled robotic planters and pickers. The majority of us are free to specialise in such trivialities as writing

---

† The concept of "economically useful" is the key to energy economics. It refers to the point at which the energy cost of doing something – whether invading a neighbouring society or sending manned flights to the moon – is lower than the energy returned or saved by the activity. Since humans are particularly bad at calculating this, time and again we engage in activities that cost more than they are worth with the result that we destroy our civilisations via the actions we take to try to sustain them.

books, building websites and optimising corporate tweets and posts to boost their appearance on social media... such, in a rather dispiriting sense, is *progress*.

The orthodoxy is a modern myth – a folk story weaved around a grain of truth in such a way that it appears plausible so long as it is not questioned too deeply. Of course a civilisation based around smartphones and fibre-optic communications is superior to anything that has gone before... or is it? In fact, the civilisation of the early twenty-first century is no longer capable of reproducing some of the technological feats of the third quarter of the twentieth. To name just two – we can no longer operate *commercial* supersonic flight. Indeed, even the jet airliners which routinely traverse the planet are some 50-100mph slower than the speeds reached at the height of global air travel in the late twentieth century – the need to conserve fuel being more important than the need to shave an extra ten minutes off an intercontinental flight. More obviously, the last human to set foot on the moon did so on 19 December 1972 – almost half a century ago. We show no sign of returning other than in the half-baked imaginations of technophile charlatans.

Nor are these leading-edge technologies the only ones to suffer. Automated car washes have become an unlikely casualty of the economic malaise that has beset the western economies in the years after the Great Financial Accident of 2008. In the UK, most independent filling stations have done away with their car washes, while supermarkets offer them only as a loss-leader (an unprofitable service that is offset when users also shop in the store). Meanwhile, a new hand car wash industry – often depending upon working conditions that amount to modern slavery – has sprung up to out-compete the more expensive (to run and, especially, maintain) automated systems.

The near-slavery of the – usually migrant – workers in hand car washes is not so far removed from the conditions for a growing army of "gig economy" workers that has exploded in the 12 years since the financial meltdown. Faced with punitive neoliberal social security systems – designed as a modern deterrent equivalent to the nineteenth century workhouse – millions of the lowest paid, least qualified and disabled workers have opted for "self-employment" which most often involves freelancing on behalf of the owners of global internet systems such as Amazon, Uber and Deliveroo. Others exist on zero-hours contracts and/or by combining several low-paid part-time jobs. And, as was intended by those who began dismantling social security in the 1980s, the presence of this "reserve army" of workers forces down the wages of those higher up the income ladder – none dare risk seeking a pay rise for fear of being fired.

The condition of working people across the so-called "developed" states speaks of something very different to *progress*. At its simplest, in 1970 a semi-skilled worker in one of the non-metropolitan regions of the UK, the USA or France could expect to earn a sufficient wage to buy a house, support a family, run a car and take an annual holiday. That same semi-skilled worker half a century later would be lucky to afford to rent a single room in a shared house. There is no way they could even dream of owning their own home, still less supporting a family, owning a car and taking a holiday. Indeed, even today's equivalents of the comfortable, suburban, semi-detached middle class households of the post-war years must have both partners in full-time middle class occupations to make ends meet. Only a shrinking metropolitan salaried class continues to enjoy a growing standard of living; blissfully unaware that the civilisation which supports them is creaking at the seams.

This is not *progress* in any sense that the majority of us would understand. Indeed, if we didn't think we knew otherwise, we would be forgiven for thinking that it looks a lot like the kind of overshoot which preceded the collapse of every other human civilisation that ever existed. Might we be in urgent need of an alternative explanation to progress and technology to understand what has happened, what is happening and what may be about to happen to our civilisation?

REFERENCE

[1] *Endgame: The Problem of Civilization.* 2006. Seven Stories Press.

ENERGY AND VALUE: THE BASICS

As the British economy industrialised during the late eighteenth and early nineteenth centuries, philosophers began to seek the causes of the apparent upsurge in wealth. At the beginning of the period, *trade* seemed to be the most obvious reason. The flow of raw materials from the American and Caribbean colonies into Britain, and the flow of manufactures from Britain out to its growing empire *appeared* to suggest that trade itself increased value.

The problem with this is that, all else being equal, in a free market trade serves to compete the prices of goods down to the cost of producing them. The kind of price gouging that occurs when a business has a monopoly or when several businesses form a cartel cannot happen in a free market simply because another business will undercut on both price and quality. And yet, nobody can deny that business owners – whether lone entrepreneurs or groups of shareholders – derived a considerable return on their investments. They wouldn't have made the investment otherwise. And that return had to come from *somewhere*.

Prior to the French Revolution, at the very apex of the system of landed agricultural estates, a group of philosophers known as the physiocrats alighted on the idea that *land* was the source of value. Later, Frederick Soddy echoed the sentiment when he suggested that "the true capitalist is a plant." That is, a plant is the only thing on the planet that can grow without the need to consume other organisms. Sunlight alone – through photosynthesis – allows plants to grow from the smallest acorns into the tallest oaks. Every other form of growth requires the consumption of other organisms *for energy*. And as we have seen, in the human case, that consumption has to be accompanied by an external energy to begin the digestive process.

For the physiocrats, the land provided the space in which plants could grow. The plants were then harvested and formed the energy base for humans and for working animals. Ergo, without the food – and the land – there could be no human activity; no economy.

Industrialisation *appeared* to turn this on its head. The productivity of the landed estates was limited. Surplus food was sufficient to support a small urban population, but no more. And ultimately the landed aristocrats lost their heads when the urban population outgrew the food surpluses that could be produced on the estates. Industrialisation, in contrast, allowed the growth of much bigger urban populations that were freed to work in increasingly large mines, foundries and manufactories producing the new goods that formed the backbone of the imperial economy.

Classical English economists like Adam Smith and David Ricardo looked elsewhere for the source of the value they saw being generated around them. If not the land, what then? According to Ricardo[1]:

> *"The value of a commodity, or the quantity of any other commodity for which it will exchange, depends on the relative quantity of labour which is necessary for its production..."*

The work carried out by a nation's labourers was what generated the value which provided a nation with its economic growth. Smith began to quantify it[2]:

> *"If among a nation of hunters, for example, it usually costs twice the labour to kill a beaver which it does to kill a deer, one beaver should naturally exchange for, or be worth two deer. It is natural that what is usually the produce of two days' or two hours' labour, should be worth double of what is usually the produce of one day's or one hour's labour."*

It fell to a later German philosopher, Karl Marx, to explain how capitalism transferred the value generated from the workers to the capitalists[3]:

> *"The values of commodities are directly as the times of labour employed in their production, and are inversely as the productive powers of the labour employed... Take the example of our spinner. We have seen that, to daily reproduce his labouring power, he must daily reproduce a value of three shillings, which he will do by working six hours daily. But this does not disable him from working ten or twelve or more hours a day. But by paying the daily or weekly value of the spinner's labouring power the capitalist has acquired the right of using that labouring power during the whole day or week."*

By paying workers a wage for the *time* they work the capitalist is able to reap the *surplus* – the amount remaining after the workers' living costs have been met – value created. This, though, was only *latent* value. It was only when and if the finished product could be sold in the marketplace that the capitalist could realise the value created. Marx set out the process as:

$$M^1 \longrightarrow C \longrightarrow M^2$$

The capitalist (or group of shareholders) invests a sum of money (M^1) into the capital, materials and wages required to produce a commodity (C) which can then be sold for a greater amount of money than was invested (M^2). The creation of value in this is simple enough for anyone to see, since the end product – a table, a bicycle or a jet airliner – is patently more useful than the raw materials used in its construction. Money, then, is merely a *measure* of the value involved – and a claim on future value – rather than a cause of value itself. The value is somehow created in the production process (C).

In effect, some factor within the productive process *has to be* paid less than the value it generates. Because of market competition, it cannot be the capital or the raw materials. It follows that the workers must be paid less than the value they provide in return. While the capitalist must pay the workers the price needed for them to "reproduce" themselves – both literally and figuratively – there is no requirement to pay the full value of the labour they provide in the course of the working week. Thus, according to Marx, profit is the unpaid labour of the working class.

Smith, Ricardo and Marx make the claim that it is labour which generates the value. This was likely more obvious to Smith, Ricardo and the early Marx – writing at a time when most of the economy ran on renewable energy – than it might have been to the later Marx, who could see the enormous power of steam-driven machinery all around him. Like the earlier physiocrats, Smith, Ricardo and the early Marx were merely observing the dominant modes of production around them and then positing the most obvious source of *some* value as being the unique source of *all* value. Indeed, in the *Grundrisse* – quite literally the "blueprint" for the proposed ten volumes of *Das Kapital* – Marx flirts with the idea that the steam driven machinery of England in the 1870s might also be a source of value. But since this would have invalidated the politics of class struggle that Marx had developed by that time, he quickly dismissed the idea again.

Marx, though, was – sort of – correct about those machines. In the modern world, this is obviously true when we look at giant robot assembly plants which produce finished goods far faster and to far higher quality than could be achieved by humans on an older production line. Contemporary Marxists have had to turn intellectual cartwheels to try to explain how these robotic plants are not actually creating value, in what amount to no more than special pleading for a Labour Theory of Value which is patently incorrect.

It isn't that labour – including intellectual labour – is not an essential component in the creation of value. After all, value is an anthropocentric concept. Rather it is that labour is but one *form* of value; and not a particularly strong one. Indeed, the key thing that makes labour a source of value is largely hidden to the observer and entirely excluded from economics textbooks: *energy*.

Most economics text books depict the economy as little more than a dance between firms and households:

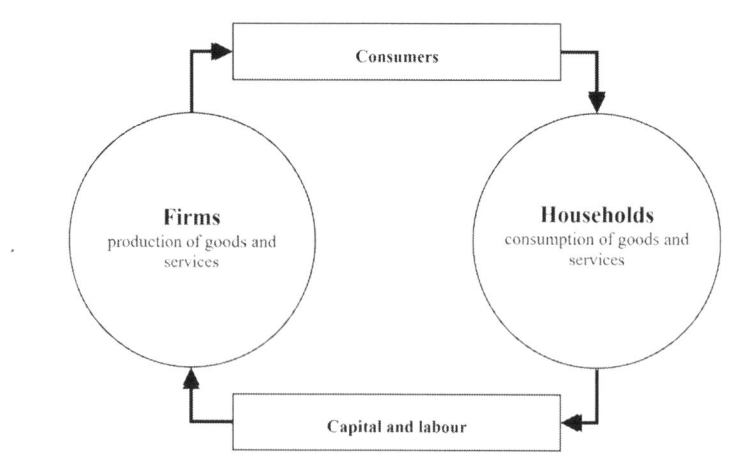

A few – particularly those with an interest in ecology – describe some of the so-called "externalities" – the raw materials, capital and labour at the beginning of the process and the pollution at the end:

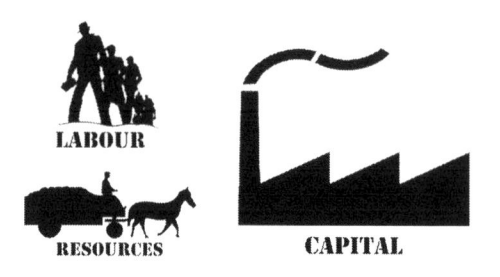

However, insofar as energy is considered at all, it – or rather the fuel from which it is generated – is regarded as just another input alongside the capital, labour and raw materials. Indeed, the fossil fuels – coal, gas and oil – which power more than 86 percent of the global economy are so cheap that they are considered far less important than the capital, labour and rarer resources like specialist alloys.

In reality, though, energy is at the beginning of everything in the economy:

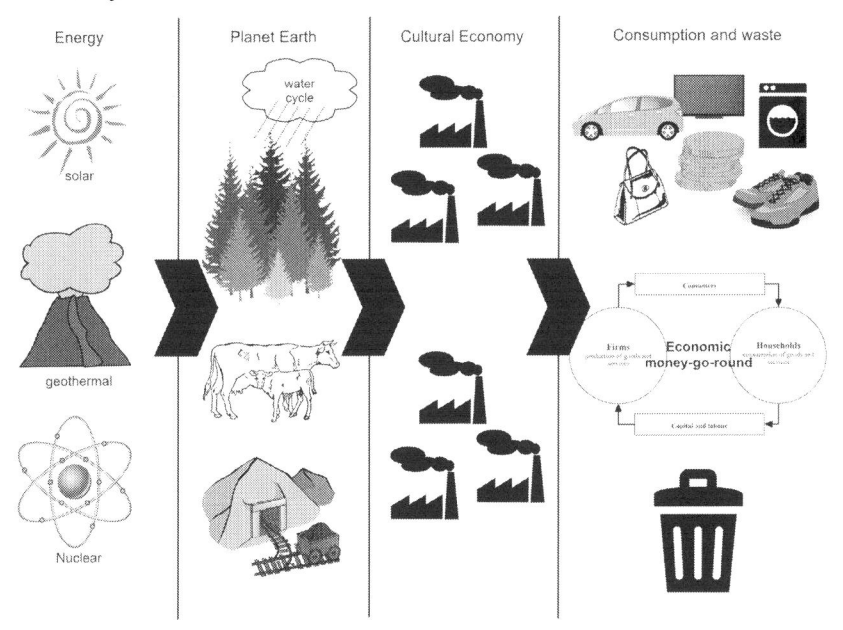

Before workers can provide labour, they must be fed. Less obviously, before raw materials can be consumed in a factory they must be harvested, mined or refined; and then transported to the factory. That takes energy at every step in the process. But energy is not paid for the value it provides to us, but merely for the cost of generating it.

Compared to machines powered by fossil fuels, human and animal labour power is weak. To match the energy provided by a single barrel of oil, a horse would have to work for roughly a year – eight hours per day, five days per week – and a human would have to work for roughly *eleven years*! Richard Heinberg offers a simpler way of understanding this: imagine your car ran out of fuel and you had to push it seven miles to the nearest filling station. How long would it take you? Most of us would struggle to push car more than a few metres. It might take the best part of a month's hard physical work to push a car seven miles. Put a litre of petrol in the tank, however, and it will take you just seven minutes. That is the difference between the energy provided by oil and the energy of human labour.

Prior to the 2020 SARS-CoV-2 pandemic, a barrel of oil was trading on world markets for around £48 ($60) per barrel. Yet that barrel of oil provided the equivalent energy output to eleven years of human work. Even at the Minimum Wage, that eleven years of work (eight hours a day, five days a week, 48 weeks per year) would cost £184,166. At the average wage it would cost £334,620. So yes, Marx was correct to infer that *some* component within the productive process was being paid *a lot* less than the value it provided. Unfortunately for him – and for generations of Marxists (and the millions who suffered and died under their tyranny) since – that *something* was not the workers.

Not that the proponents of supposedly "free" markets can take comfort from Marx's error. Understanding that energy is the source of value invalidates the various capitalist justifications for the high rates of income afforded to the owners of capital. There is nothing particularly special about them; they are mostly the heirs of people who just stumbled upon ways of deploying more energy or making production processes more energy efficient than their competitors. All else was – and is – merely an argument about the distribution of the relative shares of surplus energy.

These arguments are, however, quite literally a matter of life and death. Because human beings evolved to have an outsourced portion of our digestive system, the economy is effectively a part of our life support. Indeed, the process we call "economic growth" is little more than the increasingly complex means by which we secure the external components of our life support. There have been many blind alleys along the way, and civilisations have risen and fallen many times. But central to human life is the ongoing struggle to secure and deploy sufficient external energy to maintain ourselves.

So long as we depended upon what Soddy refers to as the Earth's revenue – the product of one year's harvest – the extent to which our species – and our economic activity – could grow was constrained by natural limits. Produce too many new babies during benign summers and we would be wiped out by famine and disease when the weather turned. Attempt to artificially raise land productivity – for example through over-irrigation or over-ploughing – and we would destroy the land in the longer-term.

What makes the modern era different is that for the first time in our collective journey, we broke into the Earth's capital store of energy. It is this – far more than idealistic theories about the European enlightenment – which explains the huge burst of productivity and economic activity which spread around the world in the centuries following the European conquest and exploitation of the Americas.

REFERENCES

[1] *The Principles of Political Economy and Taxation*, Chapter 1, Section 1.

[2] *The Wealth of Nations*, Book 1, Chapter 6.

[3] Wage-Labour and Capital/Value, Price and Profit.

THE OTHER TENDENCY FOR THE RATE OF PROFIT TO FALL

Building upon the work of classical liberal economists like Smith, Marx developed the observation that competition between firms creates the paradox of the tendency for the rate of profit to fall. That is, as firms competed with one another to bring the price of goods as low as possible, they traded a short-term gain for a long-term loss.

Central to this is Marx's concept of "socially necessary labour." This is, in effect, the number of hours – on average across the economy – required to produce a particular commodity for sale. Suppose, for example, that it takes an average of four hours' labour to make a smartphone which then sells for £400:

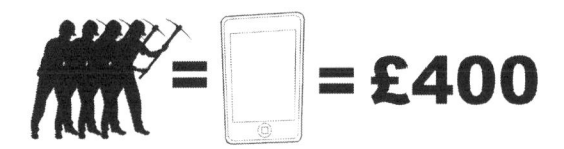

$$\text{[4 workers]} = \text{[phone]} = £400$$

Now suppose that a leading edge firm figures out a way of producing the same phone in just three hours. That firm is still able to sell the phone for £400, but if it does so, many other phone makers will still be able to compete. Instead, the firm lowers its price, passing *some* of the gain to the consumer:

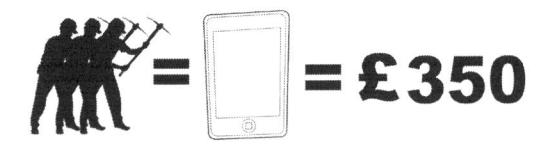

$$\text{[3 workers]} = \text{[phone]} = £350$$

Naturally, consumers are drawn to this company's phones rather than its competitors' since they get the same quality product for £50 less. In the short-term, then, despite offering the phone for £50 less, the company profits because it has cut its input costs from four to three hours' labour. In the long-term, though, competing companies will learn how to lower their own input costs until, eventually, the socially necessary labour time required to produce a phone will fall to three hours; so that the short-term advantage disappears.

It is at this point that the fundamental error made by the classical liberals and repeated by Marx leads to problems. According to the labour theory of value, since labour is the *only* source of value, by cutting the amount of labour time required to produce the phone the firm is also cutting the pool of value from which surplus (or profit) can be extracted:

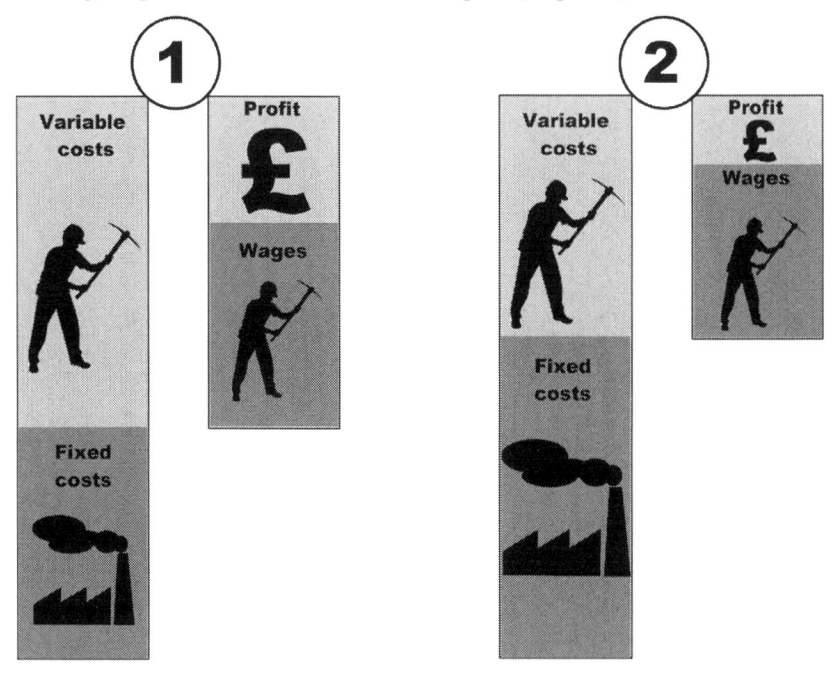

Firms have a series of fixed costs such as buildings and machinery which – according to Marx and the classical liberals – do not produce value in and of themselves, but merely allow labour to generate *more* value. Firms also have a series of variable costs, the biggest of which is the wage bill – the amount which has to be spent to allow labour to reproduce itself. The apparent paradox at the heart of capitalism is that in order to increase the value generated by labour, firms must invest in new technologies which effectively increase their fixed costs while cutting the pool of labour from which surplus value can be extracted. While firms might seek to get around this by cutting wages or by increasing the length of the working day/week, this can only mitigate the problem; it cannot overcome it.

The logical outcome – seen as impossible to eighteenth and nineteenth century economists – was that firms would eventually automate the entire production process; making it impossible for them to extract any surplus value at all. Today, though, automated assembly plants are common; causing an army of Marxian economists to turn intellectual somersaults in order to explain how they are apparently perfectly capable to continue amassing vast profits despite no longer having paid workers. In the end, though, this amounts to special pleading to avoid acknowledging a real-life situation which drives a coach and horses through the original theory.

A simpler explanation is available. This is that labour is not *the only* source of value and, indeed, has only ever been a relatively weak source of value. Energy – of which labour is but one sub-category – is the animating force which drives the economy; and it is energy which is the source of all value. And while we have never realised the nuclear engineers' promise of energy too cheap to measure, the cost of energy to firms has generally been so low as to be overlooked. Certainly the cost of energy is trivial when compared to the wage bill:

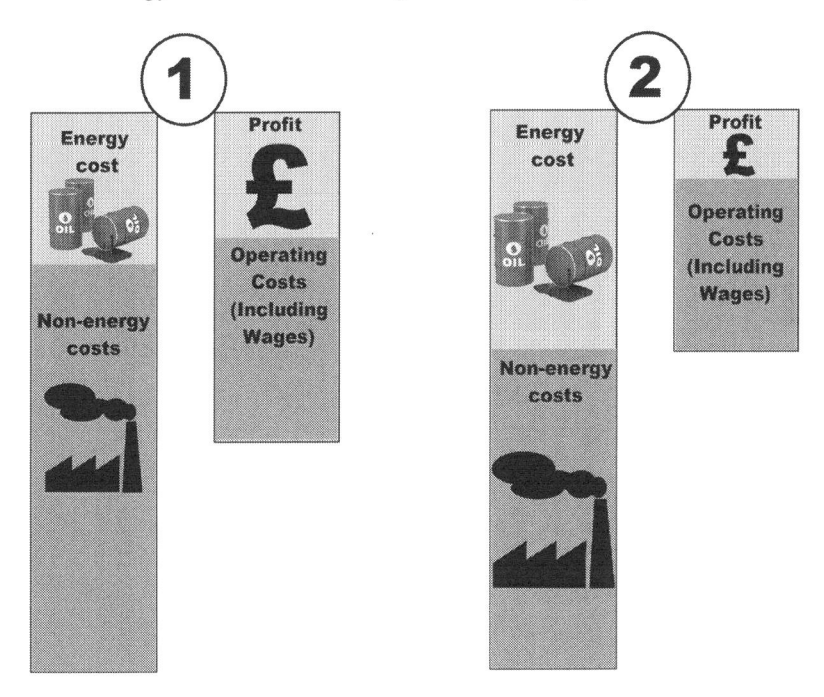

As we have seen, the way in which we exploit energy is in precisely the way Marx *believed* we exploited labour. We pay only the price of obtaining useful energy for work rather than the monetary equivalent of the value which it generates. Whether it is erecting a windmill, chopping down a tree, mining coal or drilling oil, we pay only the cost of supplying the energy. Labour, as a form of energy, is particularly expensive to obtain – at a minimum; workers must be fed, watered, clothed and housed. In pre-industrial economies, animals generated more value not just because they tend to be stronger, but also because – except in the case of slavery – the cost of maintaining them is much lower.

Industrial-scale value is primarily the result of burning the fossilised solar energy in coal, gas and oil. By combining this raw power with machinery to efficiently harness and focus it, industrial firms were able to turn workers into the machine-minders that Marx and Engels observed them to be in England by the second half of the nineteenth century. In the twentieth century, we witnessed the process move ever closer to full-automation; with the result that a large part of the population of the developed states is effectively surplus to requirement – existing only to maintain sufficient consumption to prevent the system from imploding.

As a result of the massive difference between the price of extracting and refining fossil fuels and the value which they generate, only a tiny change in the price is required to produce a major change in profitability. At the 2019 price of £48, a barrel of oil potentially provides some £335,000 worth of value. That is, for every pound spent on energy, we can generate up to £6,980 in return. If – in ordinary conditions – the price were to fall to, say, £20 per barrel – roughly the price in the boom years 1953-1973 – each pound spent on oil could generate £16,750; one reason why the post-war economy boomed while today's economy struggles to grow at all. In the event that the price increased to £80 per barrel or more – as happened in 2008 – then each pound spent on oil returns £4,187.50 or less – just a quarter of the returns made during the post-war boom.

This energy-value relationship is clouded by the more politically-charged consequences which flow from fluctuating energy prices. Because *everything* we do depends upon energy, the impact of an increase in the price is not limited to firms seeking to sell goods and services. As the price of energy rises, so does the cost of everything that we do with it. The cost of producing food, supplying water, maintaining transport infrastructure, running vehicles, heating and lighting buildings, etc. increases. This is experienced by workers and investors alike as *declining* living standards. But nobody wants to *lower* their returns to bring them into line with the new cost of energy. Indeed, it is precisely in periods when the price of energy increases that:

- Banks raise interest rates

- Investors seek higher returns
- Workers seek higher wages
- Governments seek increased taxes.

Because even an £80 barrel of oil is remarkably cheap in terms of the value it can generate, however, almost all are blind to the true reason why the economy has plunged from growth into a recession. Instead, politicians and business owners blame greedy workers and militant trade unions for the crisis. In turn, the workers blame corrupt government and greedy capitalists. Such – one way or another – has always been the struggle to obtain a share of the surplus value provided to an industrial economy by fossil fuels.

Why, though, does the price of energy fluctuate?

Oil industry investors talk about the "choke chain" effect in which supply interacts with demand to generate price. At the beginning of a price cycle there is more oil available than there is demand for it. Some is stored, but a lot is simply left in the ground as "proven reserves" – oil which could be extracted at a profit in future, but is not worth extracting immediately. As relatively cheap oil is converted by the firms which use it into surplus value, and as the surplus value is either spent or re-invested, so demand for oil increases. To begin with, the increase in demand serves to take up the existing slack in extraction. Storage facilities are slowly emptied and proven reserves are brought on stream. With profits rising, firms invest in even more production while households borrow and spend even more on consumption. There comes a time when – rather like a dog running out of lead – the spare capacity in the oil industry is exhausted. Producing even more oil at this point requires far greater investment in developing new reserves; something that will only happen if the price of oil increases. This is what happens when demand for oil in the economy overtakes supply by the industry. Oil prices increase, new resources are invested in but, paradoxically, the economy slows along with the fall in the rate of profit. Eventually the oil industry generates a surplus and the cycle repeats.

The energy industry optimises its use of energy in exactly the same way as any other business. New technologies and working practices are introduced to drive the average cost of production down. As a result, even though the *price* of oil may rise when there is a shortage of supply, and even though tapping into new reserves may be initially expensive, eventually technological improvement can drive prices down again.

This is just as well, because the bigger energy problem for industrial civilisation as a whole is that humans exploit resources on a "low-hanging fruit" basis. That is, we begin with the easiest resources and deplete these before bothering with the difficult ones. Nobody was going to dig a deep coal mine when coal seams still jutted out of the sides of Welsh hills. Nobody was going to bother drilling for oil beneath the North Sea seabed when land-based Texan wells were supplying more than enough oil to power the industrial world. Only when the oil beneath the seabed had depleted would anyone seriously consider hydraulically fracturing the source rock from which oil deposits are formed.

The 5-10 year energy choke chain cycle corresponds to the 5-10 year business cycle during which the financial economy – fuelled by cheap energy – experiences a period of growth followed by a boom or overshoot and ending in recession. There may, though, be a longer 40-60 year cycle of "Kondratiev waves" or "fourth turnings" which correspond to radical shifts in the way energy is extracted or even in the predominant type of fuel used in the economy. Investing in a new version of the existing form of fuel extraction – such as drilling a new oil well down the road from an existing one – is far less of a gamble for investors than investing in an entirely different type of extraction – such as going offshore to drill for oil beneath the seabed. Investment of this kind tends to be driven by more profound energy shortages than the ordinary ups and downs of the choke chain. For example, although the USA had begun the switch from coal to oil in the 1920s, the economies of the rest of the developed world were still predominantly coal economies. It was the slump in *net* coal energy which deepened the depression in economies like Germany, France and Britain and which helped fuel the political extremism which led to the Second World War. That war was ultimately decided by oil – the Allies had plenty; the Axis had (almost) none. In the aftermath, the developed economies – once they had rebuilt and repaired – made the switch from coal to oil at the same time as a raft of new oil fields across North Africa and the Middle East were developed; laying the ground for the biggest economic boom in human history.

It was short-lived. The first – partially artificial – oil shock in 1973 marked the end of the boom years. Apparently endless prosperity and profit was replaced by inflation, trade union militancy and investment boycotts as states, firms and workers battled one another over the relative shares of a declining value base. The post-war political settlement which had made full-employment the key aim of governments – out of fear of a return of the political extremism of the 1930s – broke down and was eventually replaced by the neoliberal focus on low-inflation. Regulations established to prevent a recurrence of the 1929 financial crash were gradually removed; freeing capital to move offshore in search of cheaper labour and higher returns. Mass unemployment became the acceptable consequence of driving inflation back below three percent.

Productivity became the order of the day. If businesses wished to remain profitable and workers wanted pay increases, they would have to increase their productivity to pay for it. For some, this involved the old capitalist trick of paying fewer workers to do more work. For others, though, it involved investment in new technologies – especially the new computers which were beginning to be mass produced – to enhance the productivity of the workforce. In this way, technology *appeared* to be the driver of productivity. In reality, productivity is intimately bound up with energy.

Productivity

In the summer of 2015 it emerged that the German car manufacturer Volkswagen had been cheating environmental protection tests; giving motorists the false idea that the cars were more fuel efficient than was actually the case. As with most other car manufacturers, from the 1990s Volkswagen had promoted diesel engines in the belief that their greater efficiency would make them more environmentally friendly than their petrol counterparts. By the start of the second decade of the twenty-first century, though, growing concern about particulate pollution from diesel vehicles had led to more stringent emissions standards which car makers like Volkswagen were obliged to respond to.

The obvious response would be to improve the engine and exhaust systems to make them more efficient and less polluting. This, though, is far easier said than done – particularly with technologies which are already at the apex of efficiency. The calculation facing managers at Volkswagen was between investing vast amounts of money to achieve tiny improvements in energy efficiency and exhaust pollution or to risk the potential costs of being caught cheating the tests. If a relatively cheap and easy technical improvement had been possible, they would have chosen the former; because there wasn't one, they chose the latter – they installed software into their cars' computer systems which could detect when a vehicle was being tested and adjust the operation of the engine accordingly.

Volkswagen was not alone in cheating, of course. Other manufacturers were caught rigging test beds or altering tyre pressures in order to give the impression that a car was travelling downhill – i.e. using less fuel – when measuring fuel efficiency. Drivers who purchased such vehicles found that they could never duplicate the promised fuel efficiency when driving on normal roads.

In the modern world, we are seldom surprised when some corporation is caught cheating, because so many corporations do it. But this was not always the case. If there had been a car manufacturer whose science and engineering team had discovered the secret sauce to make diesel engines and exhaust systems more efficient without bankrupting the company, they would have advertised the fact while exposing their competitors' cheating. They would very likely have lobbied governments to make regulations *even tougher* in order to put their competitors out of business. This, after all, is how small companies used to become giant corporations in decades gone by.

We are late in the energy game today; and the car industry is experiencing the same decline that is affecting the global economy as a whole. Indeed, the current interest in switching to electric – or possibly hydrogen – cars marks a shift from attempting to improve the efficiency of internal combustion engines to a new power source which trades performance for saving energy. It is the same process which has reduced the speed of air travel by 50-100mph in the last twenty years. The quest for speed – most notably in the Anglo-French *Concorde* – has been replaced by a demand for lean-burn/energy-efficient engines that help keep the cost of air travel down by increasing journey times.

This happens with any technology. The 1903 *Wright Flyer* is a world apart from the supersonic *Concorde* in the same way that Gresley's *Mallard* travelling at 126mph in 1936 is a world apart from Trevithick's bone-shaking 1804 engine rattling its way down the Taff valley at 15 mph (and having to be pulled back with horses). They are, though, merely different versions of the same technologies. Once Trevithick and the Wright brothers had demonstrated that the technologies were viable, engineers and technologists piled in to improve the design; making small and low-cost technical changes that led to big improvements in performance. By the time we arrive at the *Mallard/Concorde* stage, though, the technology is itself so expensive that it needs a government subsidy to make it *economically* viable. But this, in turn, makes it *politically* unacceptable – subsidised travel inevitably becomes exclusive travel for the rich and famous; something that ordinary workers resent paying taxes to support:

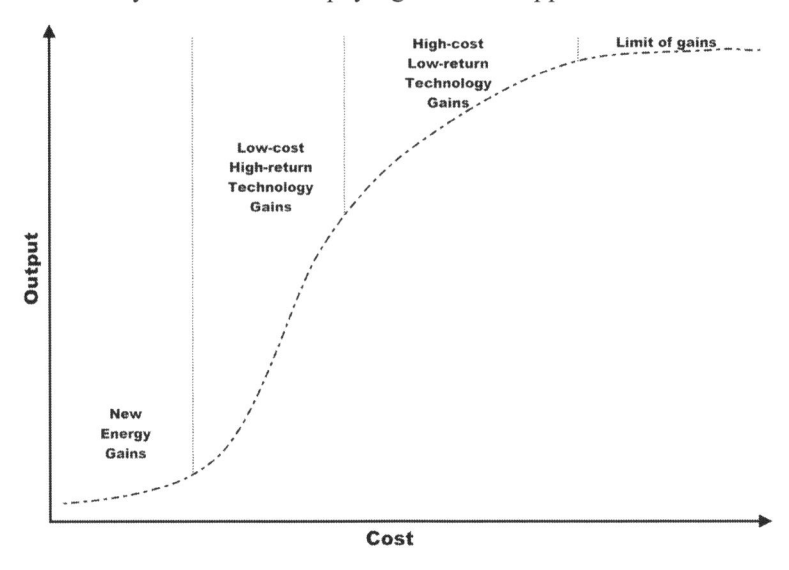

We are conditioned – by the underlying myth of progress which underpins all western ideologies – to think of the human trajectory as being ever onward and upward in a straight line of progress which will lead, ultimately, to our metastasising across the galaxy. In reality, though, progress – insofar as it happens at all – undulates in line with the volume and source of energy available to us. This was obvious enough through millennia of pre-industrial living during which prosperity and decline were intimately linked to the climate via food growth. A period of benign seasons would produce food surpluses which allowed for growing prosperity and population growth. A change of climate or a "mini ice age," in contrast, would result in poverty and malnutrition which would ultimately lead to the arrival of the Biblical horsemen; famine, pestilence, war and death.

The industrial age has been different because instead of limiting our activities to the products of the annual solar energy landing on the planet in one growing season, we drilled into a store of millions of years of sunlight concentrated into the fossil carbons coal, gas and oil. These allowed us to create technologies that would have seemed like magic to our pre-industrial ancestors. Even magic wears thin, however. As physicist Tom Murphy explained in an essay called *You Call this Progress?*[1]:

> "Let's set the stage with a thought experiment about three equally-separated times, centered around 1950. Obviously we will consider the modern epoch—2015. The symmetric start would then be 1885, resulting in 65-year interval comparisons: roughly a human lifetime.
>
> "So imagine magically transporting a person through time from 1885 into 1950—as if by a long sleep—and also popping a 1950 inhabitant into today's world. What an excellent adventure! Which one has a more difficult time making sense of the updated world around them? Which one sees more 'magic,' and which one has more familiar points of reference? The answer is obvious, and is essentially my entire point.
>
> "Take a moment to let that soak in, and listen for any cognitive dissonance popping inside your brain.
>
> "Our 19th Century rube would fail to recognize cars/trucks, airplanes, helicopters, and rockets; radio, and television (the

telephone was 1875, so just missed this one); toasters, blenders, and electric ranges. Also unknown to the world of 1885 are inventions like radar, nuclear fission, and atomic bombs. The list could go on. Daily life would have undergone so many changes that the old timer would be pretty bewildered, I imagine. It would appear as if the world had blossomed with magic: voices from afar; miniature people dancing in a little picture box; zooming along wide, hard, flat roads at unimaginable speeds—much faster than when uncle Billy's horse got into the cayenne pepper. The list of 'magic' devices would seem to be innumerable.

"Now consider what's unfamiliar to the 1950 sleeper. Look around your environment and imagine your life as seen through the eyes of a mid-century dweller. What's new? Most things our eyes land on will be pretty well understood. The big differences are cell phones (which they will understand to be a sort of telephone, albeit with no cord and capable of sending telegram-like communications, but still figuring that it works via radio waves rather than magic), computers (which they will see as interactive televisions), and GPS navigation (okay: that one's thought to be magic even by today's folk). They will no doubt be impressed with miniaturization as an evolutionary spectacle, but will tend to have a context for the functional capabilities of our gizmos.

"Telling ourselves that the pace of technological transformation is ever-increasing is just a fun story we like to believe is true. For many of us, I suspect, our whole world order is built on this premise."

The coal-powered steam technologies that transformed the world in the nineteenth century were developed and improved to the point that they reached their peak efficiency in the early decades of the twentieth. By this time, though, a more energy-dense and easier stored alternative – oil – had arrived on the scene. This allowed the further development of some steam technologies, the redundancy of others, and the development of several new ones. But the reason our twenty-first century technologies would still be understandable to someone from 1950 is that they are merely *updated versions* of existing technologies.

The issue facing us today is that many technologies have passed an energetic peak – we have squeezed maximum performance from them, but have discovered that the costs of doing so are too great. As an example, Commander Eugene Cernan was the last human to stand on the moon. That was nearly half a century ago in December 1972. Since then, the best any human has done is to travel to very low Earth orbit on scientific, commercial and (one assumes) military missions. It is not that we somehow lost the blueprints to the Apollo rockets or, indeed, that we haven't figured out how to improve on them. What has changed is that the energy cost of sending missions to what turned out to be a barren rock is too costly for the wider economy to bear. And so rockets to the moon have gone the same way as supersonic commercial flight and 126mph steam locomotives.

The problem stems from the laws of thermodynamics. In any process which turns energy from one form into another, a portion of that energy is lost as waste heat. Worse still, when it comes to human technologies, a large part of the energy is lost as waste heat. Think, for example, of how hot your car engine and exhaust pipe gets as you drive along; so much so that we need a separate cooling system to transfer some of the waste heat from the engine to a radiator where it will be dispersed by the air flowing through it. In an ideal world there would be no heat loss at all. Instead, all of the energy stored in the petrol would be converted into motion; propelling the car as efficiently as possible.

The energy density of a fuel sets a hard boundary on what we can do with it. The energy density of charcoal, for example, is about 4,300 k calories[†] per kilogramme. In practice, of course, we would only get a fraction of that as useful – "*exergy*"[*]– work. The rest would be lost as waste heat. We might improve our technology. For example, a charcoal oven might be better insulated to prevent heat escaping and we might add bellows to pump more oxygen into the reaction. But like it or not, if we want more energy from each unit of fuel, we need to switch fuels. Coal, at around 6,000 kcals per Kg, would provide us with a lot more energy. So much so, indeed, that it might allow us to convert water into steam to power machinery. Oil, at around 10,000 kcals per Kg, gives us an even bigger bang for our buck. Indeed, because it is liquid, it is far easier to store; making it much better as a transport fuel.

[†] A calorie is the amount of energy required to raise the temperature of a gram of water by one degree Celsius.

[*] In thermodynamics, the exergy of a system is the maximum useful work possible during a process that brings the system into equilibrium with a heat reservoir, reaching maximum entropy.

The easiest way to increase the work generated from an energy source would be to increase the amount of the fuel used – shovelling additional coal into the furnace or increasing the capacity of an internal combustion engine. There is, for example, a big difference between a 50cc moped and a 1000cc superbike – primarily the amount of fuel flowing into the engine at any time. Changing to a more energy-dense fuel would also make a difference – diesel trains, for example, accelerate faster and maintain higher speeds than steam trains. But changing fuels involves a high conversion cost because of the prior investment in the technology for the less energy-dense fuel. This is where *productivity* – getting more work from an existing energy input or getting the same work from less energy input – is important.

Imagine that your family own a widget making company. In the days before industrialisation, your company would provide the tools and materials for making widgets to a number of freelance workers who would be paid for the number of widgets they made. As the Atlantic trade increases, though, there is greater demand for widgets than your workers can provide. Worse still, there are no more workers to hire. And so your company decides to invest in the new water-powered widget-making machinery. At around 0.5kcals per litre, the water that runs down the steep and narrow valley to your new factory provides far more useful energy than your workers alone could ever have done. And over time, with improved materials and lubricants, the machinery converts the maximum possible water-power into work.

This improvement, however, pales in comparison to another productivity improvement made at this time. Instead of having each worker make a widget of his own, you arrange the workers and machinery so that each repeats a single step in the process of making a widget. This "production line" technique allows you to make the best use of the water-power; producing more widgets than you could have hoped for; and making your company prosperous in the process.

The Atlantic trade in widgets, though, is never content. And as the global market expands, there is far more demand for widgets than even your water-powered production line-based factory can provide. Adding water to the flow is not within your gift; and in any case, too much water would damage the machinery. You might make some additional tweaks to the machinery, but as you are operating close to the thermodynamic limit, this will provide little additional work and will come at an unacceptably high cost. The same goes for reorganising the production line; which is likely to upset workers who will then need to be placated with higher wages. There is nothing for it other than to change your energy source.

Fortunately, engineers have taken the basic ideas from the beams, wheels and gears used in water-powered machinery and have found a way to drive them using pressurised steam. In addition to providing more work, these steam engines have the advantage of being constant. They allow manufacturing to continue during periods of drought and they don't put the machinery at risk from floods.

The cost of the new steam technology will quickly be repaid from the profits returned from the sale of additional widgets. And then, over time, the productivity process is repeated. Improvements are made to the technology allowing the maximum conversion of coal/steam-power into work. New work arrangements are made in order to make full use of the additional energy; allowing the production of widgets to peak once more. And once again, as the thermodynamic limits are reached, additional productivity gains can only be made at a very high cost for a very small improvement; so that eventually further improvement isn't worth it.

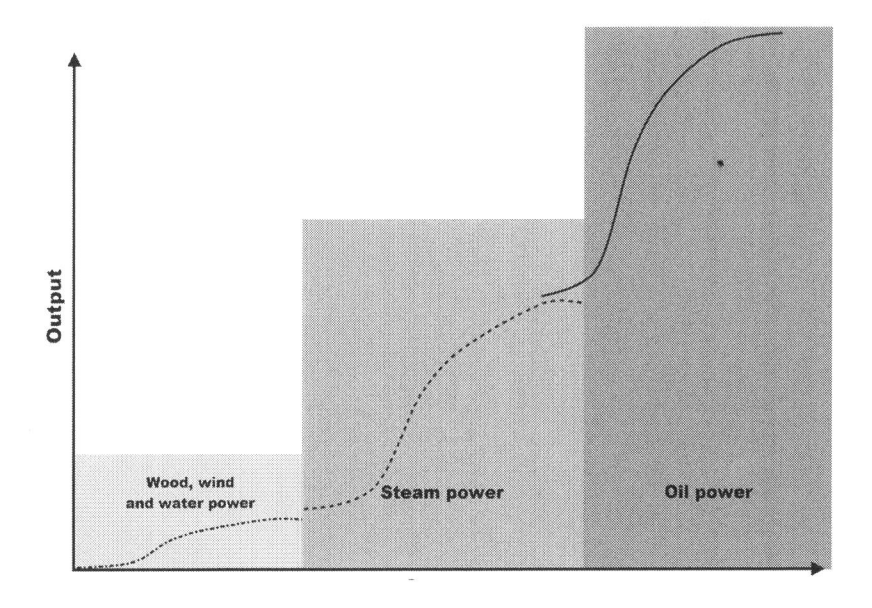

As demand continues to grow, your company makes a final switch to diesel fuel – at around 9,500 kcals per litre – to power the widget manufacturing process. And one last time, the productivity process repeats. Machinery is optimised and working arrangements altered in order to convert as much energy as possible into useful work. And once again, thermodynamic limits are reached – additional improvements to the technology and changes to working arrangements can only provide limited gains in output and come at too high a price to make them worthwhile.

At this point, energy-efficiency becomes more important than productivity. That is, it is better to produce fewer widgets using less energy than it would be to go full tilt at producing as many widgets as possible. It is for this reason that so many modern companies talk about "going green" or working toward being "carbon-neutral" – not out of concern for the environment, but simply because the cost of further productivity gains is far too high.

REFERENCE

[1] "You Call this Progress?" 2015. *Do the Math* blog. https://dothemath.ucsd.edu/2015/09/you-call-this-progress

A Brief Alternative History of the Industrial Age

The late sixteenth century witnessed a massive change in England which is still visible in the surviving architecture from the period. A visitor to the British Isles today will still find plenty of Tudor period timber-framed buildings:

Gradually, beginning with the palaces of the rich, but extending to dwellings throughout the country, bricks and mortar began to replace timber as the main building material. This was more than mere fad. Although brick construction had been regarded as an expensive luxury, by the beginning of the seventeenth century it was becoming a necessity.

King James VI of Scotland – who was to succeed Elizabeth as James I of England – is reputed to have said of his native Edinburgh that had the Easter story taken place there, Judas would have found no tree from which to hang himself. Historian Clive Ponting documents a major timber shortage which plagued Western Europe at that time:

> *"A timber shortage was first noticed in Europe in specialised areas such as shipbuilding... In the 1580s when Philip II of Spain built the armada to sail against England and the Dutch had to import timber from Poland... Local sources of wood and charcoal were becoming exhausted – given the poor state of communications and the costs involved it was impossible to move supplies very far.*

As early as 1560 the iron foundries of Slovakia were forced to cut back production as charcoal supplies began to dry up. Thirty years later the bakers of Montpellier in the South of France had to cut down bushes to heat their ovens because there was no timber left in their town..."

In the decades after the Black Death decimated somewhere between a third and two-thirds of the population of Europe, benign climactic conditions transformed recovery into a thriving population which gradually overshot its land base. In an economy which depended upon wood both as a fuel source – either directly or as charcoal – and as a key building material, over-consumption of forests and woods was devastating.

Although backward in comparison to the Ottoman and Ming Empires which ruled their respective regions of the planet at that time, Western Europe was made up of a patchwork of kingdoms, duchies and city states which competed against each other and combined against the emergence of any one dominant state in a complex dance of war and trade. The Hapsburg Empire was the dominant European power of the day. But the rest of Europe periodically acted against the Hapsburgs to prevent dominance from becoming total. Nevertheless, the state which built 130 warships to sail against Perfidious Albion in 1588 was not to be trifled with.

And yet the apparently inferior English had warships of their own; and skilled seamen to crew them. And while they could not defeat the Armada in a set piece battle, knowledge of local tides and the use of commando tactics caused the Spanish to effectively defeat themselves; forcing them to sail around the British Isles where many of the remaining warships came to grief in the treacherous North Atlantic seas.

As sociologist Immanuel Wallerstein explains, military conflict was a founding feature of the "modern world system" which originated in Western Europe at this time. That competition put England at a particular disadvantage as naval power began to emerge as the most important branch of the military. With timber supplies – particularly the long beams needed to construct warships – dwindling, Eastern Europe was the only reliable source. But accessing the same Polish timber used by the Spanish to construct the Armada was risky for their English foe. The Baltic Sea was a potential trap for any English fleet foolish enough to sail into it. It would have been all too easy for a hostile fleet to blockade the exit route through the narrow straits between Sweden and Denmark. And so the English were forced to look further afield for their timber. This meant taking the route around the North Cape – a route still considered dangerous to modern shipping – to access Russian timber.

To make the round trip with even a margin of safety, English ship building had to go through a revolution. The earlier ships that had sailed the shallow waters around the British coast were too fragile to cope with North Atlantic storms. And so new designs and new methods of ship building were devised to allow the construction of larger and sturdier ocean-going ships. It was on these ships that English captains like Francis Drake developed the seamanship that was to defeat the Armada in 1588.

The Spanish, of course, had ocean-going ships of their own at this point; their sailors being the first to discover and the settle colonies in the Caribbean from the 1490s. These expeditions were initially regarded as failures due to a miscalculation of the size of the circumference of the planet. Medieval Europe had paid a high price for luxury goods like spices and silk transported along the Silk Road from Asia across the Russian Steppe into Europe. At each stage along the journey, some landowner, duke or king would impose a duty upon the goods flowing across his land. And every time the goods were traded between merchants along the route, a modest profit was taken. The result was that by the time these goods reached the backward fringes of Western Europe they were too expensive for all but the richest to afford. The fifteenth century "Voyages of Discovery" were an attempt by the Atlantic-facing European states to break the monopoly by finding a direct route to the Asian states where the luxury goods were produced. The Portuguese had already discovered the route east around Cape Hope and through the Straits of Malacca. On their return they were able to make profits thousands of times the initial investment while still selling luxury goods for a fraction of the prevailing price. So it fell to their Spanish competitors to seek a western route. This is why the Italian, Columbus, was hired by the Spanish crown to discover the best western passage to "The Indies" (the term used to describe the entire of Southeast Asia at the time). What no living European knew at that point was that the Earth was far larger and that there was a huge landmass to the west between them and Asia.

Columbus was fortunate insofar as he discovered *some* gold in the Caribbean islands that he mapped out. But the real treasures of the Americas were to be found years later when the Spanish moved into Central and South America. The Portuguese might have found the best sea route to the Indies, but with gold and silver from the Americas, the Spanish could buy as many luxuries as they chose. That, at least, was the theory.

Gold has a number of properties that make it particularly attractive to humans. It is rare, which gives it a scarcity value. It is sometimes referred to as "the eternal metal" as it doesn't oxidise and so does not decay over time. It is incredibly heavy in comparison to most other substances. And it takes considerable effort to obtain. All of which make it attractive as a measure of value for trade purposes. The Spanish, though, made the same mistake that economists, bankers and kings continue to make today. They mistook a *measure* of value for value itself.

Like all forms of currency, gold acted as a means of transferring value from the present to the future. That is, a merchant might trade goods for a quantity of gold. But this was only done so that the gold could be exchanged for something of equivalent value later on. Even state treasuries which appeared to hoard gold did so only to fund the next war or emergency, while hoping that the gold would be an insurance against something that didn't happen rather than a payment for something which did.

In a settled economy such as that across Eurasia in the years prior to 1500, the supply of gold was relatively stable. Moreover, since most ordinary people continued to operate on a non-monetary basis – using devices like tally sticks to keep a record of debts and favours – there had been little inflationary pressure within the economy. Kings and bankers were always tempted into adulterating the currency – also a practice that is institutionalised today – by clipping coins or adding base metal to the gold and silver. No amount of adulteration, however, could come close to the inflation that was unleashed by the influx of gold and silver from the Americas.

The problem was that the new gold was not accompanied by the generation of an equivalent amount of value in what we would today call "the real economy." Indeed, the timber shortages that had already become an economic problem for the people of Europe actively prevented the generation of additional value. Even investing some of the new gold in new economic activities couldn't solve the problem because the wood and charcoal required for the new activity could only be obtained by depriving an existing activity.

When new currency enters an economy without an equivalent real value being generated, the initial *apparent* wealth rapidly turns into its opposite. Competing for the same value, the holders of the new currency effectively bid up the price of everything they seek to buy. One consequence of this is a process of social dislocation as the classes at the base of society witness their prosperity plummet, while factions within the upper echelons begin to fall from grace. In the case of the Spanish Hapsburgs, this gave rise to revolt and the loss of lands in the Netherlands together with a fracturing of the Empire into its Spanish and Austrian parts.

Spain's (and Portugal's) loss was to be someone else's gain. The three other nations which set sail to the new (to Europeans) lands across the Atlantic – the Dutch, French and English – found something far more valuable than the gold and silver prised by the Iberian states. Rather than metals that were but a claim on wealth, these three states found wealth itself; not least in the virgin forests of North America.

In Euro-centric histories, the Voyages of Discovery and the conquest and colonisation of the Americas are often presented as just the latest episode on the long upward wave of progress from Ancient Greece to the stars. It was, they tell us, a combination of scientific thinking and technological superiority which propelled the Europeans across the Atlantic. In reality, it was something far more mundane.

The Ming Empire of the period was fully capable of building ocean-going ships that would likely have been superior to their European equivalents had they ever met in battle. Their trade ships, too, were capable of making the round trip to the Americas. What prevented the Ming Chinese from conquering and colonising the Americas, and paved the way for the Europeans, was renewable *energy* – solar and gravitational:

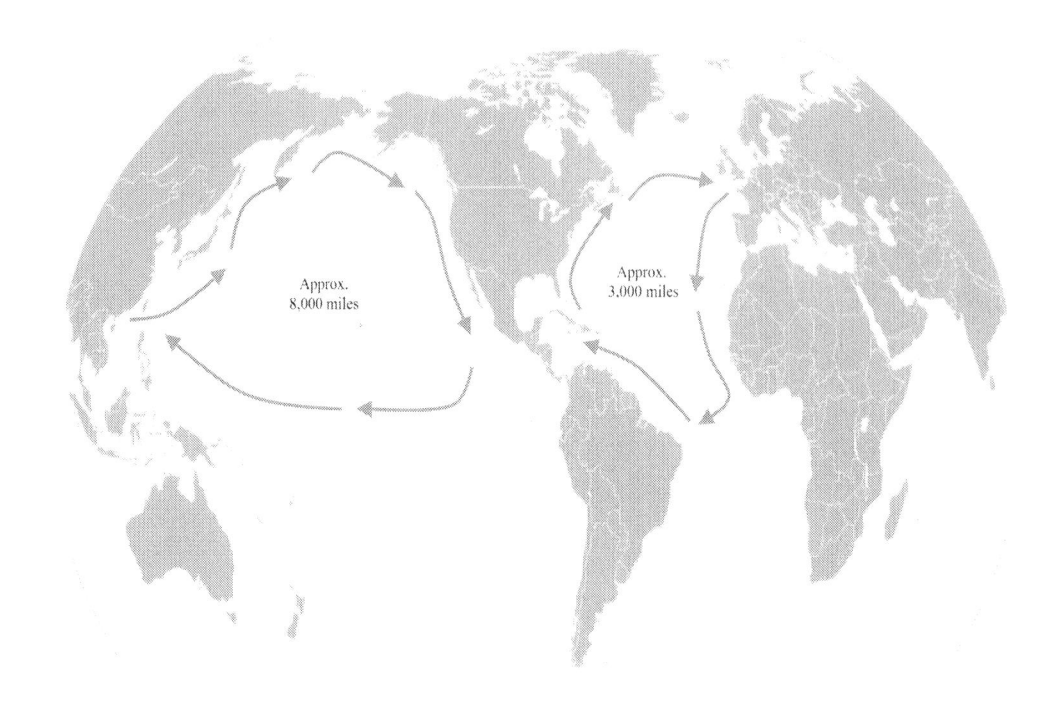

The sailing ships of the period relied on favourable winds and ocean gyres to propel them across the oceans. This gave the Europeans a big advantage over the Chinese. The best route for crossing the Atlantic from Europe to America was to follow the African coast near to the Equator before swinging west toward the coast of Brazil and then following the coast of South America west to the Caribbean. The best return route was to sail north to the Eastern seaboard of North America before swinging east back to Europe. This gave an ocean crossing of around 3,500 miles. The best route from Asia across the Pacific would require a trip of some 8,000 miles north along the Siberian coast and then across the Bering Strait to Alaska before following the West Coast of America south to Mexico before heading west for the return journey. One consequence was that while a Ming ship of the period could be loaded with sufficient supplies to make the journey, the space left on European ships after provisioning for the round trip was sufficient to plant a colony.

That the Europeans were motivated by the pursuit of wealth, together with a cultural desire to spread Christianity (at the end of a musket if need be) is without question. It was, however, the accident of the Earth's currents and trade winds that allowed them to succeed.

Spanish and Portuguese settlement in the Americas began almost immediately after Columbus's voyages, with several colonies established by the end of the first decade of the sixteenth century. English efforts were less successful. Although English sailors had made the round trip to North America under John Cabot in 1497, attempted colonies at Roanoke and Newfoundland failed. Nevertheless, by the seventeenth century, it was the English and French who were to emerge as the main colonisers in North America and as major landholders in South America and the Caribbean.

Although Europeans have tended to delude themselves into believing that sixteenth century America was a virgin land, the reality is that centuries of cultivation by the indigenous people had made large parts of the Americas ideal for growing a variety of foods without which the European colonists would have starved. More importantly for the development of the modern world, those fertile soils could be turned over to the farming of crops which massively boosted the economies of Europe.

The humble potato brought a big increase in calories to the peoples of Europe. Turnips did the same for livestock. Prior to the introduction of root crops from the Americas, most European livestock had to be slaughtered in winter. An abundance of root vegetables to see both humans and animals through the lean winter months allowed many more animals to be kept alive; allowing much greater access to protein.

Raw calories were also delivered in the form of sugar cones refined from the sugar cane that plantations across the Caribbean and South America were growing in quantities undreamed of by fifteenth century Europeans. As Jonathan Hersh and Hans-Joachim Voth report[2]:

> *"While medieval Cyprus produced no more than an estimated 50-100 tons of sugar per year, Santo Domingo in the 18th century alone produced 3,500 tons. England in 1700 imported approximately 10,000 tons; a century later, this figure had risen to 150,000 tons, according to some estimates…*
>
> *"The discoveries made life better by offering access to sugar, tea, chocolate, tobacco, and coffee. Aggregate consumption of these colonial luxuries grew rapidly during the early modern period. Starting either from zero (for tea, tobacco, and coffee) or from very low levels of consumption (sugar), English imports per head surged*

to 23 pounds of sugar, almost 2 pounds of tea, 1 pound of tobacco, and 0.1 pound of coffee by 1804-06."

The impact of this Atlantic trade cannot be overstated. On the negative side of the equation, an additional energy source was added to the wind and tides which powered the ships of the period. Human labour in its most basic and brutal form – slavery – became the means by which the price of the raw materials brought back from the Americas was kept to a minimum.

On the outbound leg of this "Triangular Trade," Europeans would exchange goods – including weapons – with one group of Africans in exchange for some of their enslaved African neighbours. These slaves (derived from the word "Slav" from the days when Middle Eastern empires would enslave people from the Balkans) would be shipped across the Atlantic to sell as replacements for the slaves that had been worked to death on the plantations. On the third leg of the journey, ships would be loaded up with goods and raw materials – notably cotton – for delivery to the home economy, where they would be sold for consumption or converted into finished goods in the burgeoning manufactories of the period.

The psychoactive products – tobacco, chocolate and coffee – together with the sugar were to have a profound impact on the minds of the Europeans who consumed them. For example, Angela Jansz and Tracey Taylor argue that[3]:

> *"Prior to Spanish exploration of the Americas, Europe of the old world had a very limited repertoire of psychoactive substances. There was no opium, caffeine (in the form of tea or coffee), no tobacco or cannabis and the native European solenaceous hallucinogens and other herbs used in healing were enmeshed in superstition or dispensed with limited understanding by apothecaries.*
>
> *"There really was only one psychoactive drug, alcohol. It had to fulfil a wide range of social, medicinal and intoxicating functions."*

Tom Standage explains that[4]:

> *"The impact of the introduction of coffee into Europe during the seventeenth century was particularly noticeable since the most*

common beverages of the time, even at breakfast, were weak 'small beer' and wine. ... Those who drank coffee instead of alcohol began the day alert and stimulated, rather than relaxed and mildly inebriated, and the quality and quantity of their work improved. ... Western Europe began to emerge from an alcoholic haze that had lasted for centuries."

It is no accident that the European Enlightenment began in the Coffee Houses of England and the (coffee-drinking) Salons of France. But it was the additional energy source – the calories from the massive influx of sugar – which freed people's minds to ponder the deeper mysteries of the world around them.

Once again, the development of our modern world system rested more on accident than some pre-ordained upward arc of progress. Nevertheless, progress of sorts it was for we naked apes whose digestion is partially outsourced. And as always, good is never good enough. The demand for more and better drove us into conflict – notably the Age of Revolutions and the Napoleonic Wars which followed.

The American Revolution has passed into history as a supreme folly of a detached English ruling elite. There was absolutely no need to levy taxes and duties upon the American colonies to pay for the earlier war with France; save for a point of principle. Indeed, Parliamentarians at the time warned that the cost of collecting the proposed taxes and duties would be greater than the revenues returned to England. Less obviously, though, the American colonies had broken a key – but unwritten – rule of the Empire: only England can manufacture goods.

This was the fourth – hidden – leg of the erroneously named triangular trade. The cotton that was returned from the American plantations was turned into finished cloth in the water-powered factories of Lancashire. The finished cotton cloth was considered almost as good – and as valuable – as silk when contrasted with the woollen garments which preceded it. But in order to make the system function (to the advantage of the English elite) the colonies had to be prevented from weaving their own cotton cloth. The same went for the growing range of goods being manufactured in a rapidly industrialising Britain.

That economists like Adam Smith could see trade as the foundation of the wealth of nations was solely because he happened to be based in Britain. That fourth trade leg, which sold manufactured goods back to the outposts of empire, was little more than a wealth pump for extracting the wealth of the colonies. When the British began doing the same thing to India, the sub-continent was among the wealthiest places on Earth. By the time the British left in 1947, India was among the poorest.

The American colonists saw through the trick though. One of the forces behind the American Revolution was the growth of manufacturing in the Thirteen Colonies. It was this as much as the desire for compensation for defeating the French which put the British elite on a collision course with their colonial subjects.

What makes England unusual in the history of human Empires is that it managed to repeat the trick. Ordinarily, the loss of the important American colonies would have signalled the beginning of the end of the British Empire. And yet a century after the defeat, Britain stood as the world's first truly global Empire – one which contained a quarter of the world's population and a land area so big that the sun never set over it.

If cotton was the backbone of the British Empire 1.0, then coal was the foundation of British Empire 2.0. Originally regarded as an inferior fuel to wood and charcoal because of the damage it caused to hearths and furnaces, coal was readily available in regions of Great Britain that had already begun to power manufacturing with water power. Although only a fraction more "energy dense" than charcoal[†], coal was immediately available; with seams often protruding from the sides of hills such as those along the Severn Gorge where the world's first iron bridge was constructed at the same time as Britain was losing the American War of Independence.

There was as much potential energy in the form of coal beneath Great Britain as there was in oil beneath Saudi Arabia; and Britain's exploitation of it was to follow a pattern copied by the latter. This is sometimes called "the low-hanging fruit" pattern of exploitation. The first exploited coal could be simply gouged out of the side of hills. Elsewhere, deposits could be exploited by digging simple pits. Only when these first deposits were exhausted were miners forced to go underground and to dig ever deeper.

One way of looking at this progression was that increasing energy – either direct or embodied in additional technologies – had to be invested

---
† Around 35 megajoules per kilogramme (MJ/Kg) compared to 30 MJ/Kg

in order to continue exploiting the energy source. But it was not just the additional energy required to dig deeper which caused problems. Toxic gas was an ever-present danger to miners and mines alike – providing us with the contemporary saying, "the canary in the mine." Miners used songbirds as an early warning of the build-up of gas; when the canary stopped singing it was time to flee. Water, too, could be a major problem for deep mining. In shallow pits and mines, oxen or work horses could be used to power rudimentary pumps for bringing excess water to the surface. In deeper mines, water built up faster than animals could pump it. To overcome the problem, miners turned to the raw technology that was to propel the world into the fossil fuel age: the steam-powered beam engine.

The early industrial age (1750-1850) witnessed an order of magnitude growth in UK coal production from around 4.25 million tons to nearly 51 million tons[5]. This, however, was only the beginning of industrial civilisation's voracious demand for energy. By 1913 – the year British coal production peaked – the UK was producing nearly 322 million tons of coal[6] to power its domestic industry and to supply a massive navy to police an empire that encompassed a quarter of the world.

This technology followed a similar – low-hanging fruit – process in which the early examples were energy-inefficient; converting far too much of the coal and steam into waste heat rather than motive power. A series of relatively simple improvements made beam engines far more energy efficient, minimising the amount of coal that had to be burned to prevent a mine from flooding. At a certain stage, however, diminishing returns set in – each new improvement cost more while the energy-efficiency gain was ever smaller.

The beam engine, nevertheless, paved the way for a series of innovations in transport that genuinely revolutionised the economy. The development of steam-powered locomotives allowed the separation of extraction and manufacturing for the first time. Firms that wanted to operate coal-powered factories could be located closer to their markets or to ports, while railways could move the coal from the coalfields to the factory towns. As with the beam engine, locomotives took time to develop. Nevertheless, they were the same basic technology; and it was the simple, early improvements – improved sleepers, angled wheels, stronger axles, etc. – which made railways a viable industry.

The opening of the Liverpool to Manchester *public* railway in 1830 is usually given as the beginning of the British railway industry – although, as we have seen, steam-powered *private* railways predate this; including Stephenson's Stockton and Darlington Railway, which opened in 1825. The expansion of the railway network thereafter came in fits and starts resulting from financial speculation creating a series of booms and busts. As Leigh Shaw-Taylor and Xuesheng You explain[7]:

> *"Following the Liverpool and Manchester Railway, there was a forty-year period of railway construction on a massive scale... At the end of 1830, there were just over 125 miles of railway lines in Britain yet, by the end of 1871, this figure had jumped to more than 13,000 miles. Railway expansion did not proceed at an even pace over this time. In contrast, there were three separate periods of intensive and speculative railway promotion, investment and construction; known as the 'railway manias' these periods occurred in the late-1830s, the mid-1840s and the early-1860s."*

Just as coal mining gave birth to the steam technology which gave birth to steam railways, so the expansion of the railways allowed for the further expansion of coal mining itself. For example[7]:

> *"While it is easy to appreciate the importance of a nationwide network with long distance routes and wide geographical coverage, we should not dismiss the economic significance of some local railway lines that had not yet been connected to a wider network. A good example is the Taff Valley railway line that connected the Welsh coalfield with the port of Cardiff.*

> *"Even though the Taff Valley Railway was less than 30 miles long, it is difficult to exaggerate its impact. Before the arrival of railways, canals monopolised coal transportation in South Wales. The limited capacity and speed of canals placed a cap on the development of the South Wales coal industry. The construction of the Taff Valley Railway from Cardiff to Merthyr in 1840-41 effectively ended the canal companies' monopoly of coal transportation in the region...*

> *"From 1856 to 1864, the decade after the Rhondda valley was linked with the Taff Valley Railway, output from its coalfield more than doubled – from 205,200 tons to 520,022 tons; by 1869, coal production reached 1,250,000 tons and, by the mid-1880s, it had risen to more than 5,500,000 tons. Accompanying the exponential*

expansion of the coal mining industry, was a boom in population. Rhondda's population in 1831 was just over 1,500 and during the next 80 years it grew 100-fold to reach more than 150,000 in 1911."

Steam revolutionised sea travel too. A new generation of steam-powered ships allowed the transportation of goods against the wind. For the first time it became possible to run a timetable of shipping between Europe and America (albeit a timetable with a lot of built-in leeway). A state which operated steam ships also had access to a network of global trade that was barely accessible to states which still depended upon renewable energy. More importantly, though, a state which had control of the world's coal ports could control the trade flows of every steam-powered merchant fleet. Most of all, a state with a big enough steam-powered navy could control the coal ports and the sea trade routes around the planet. And in an age in which travel around continents was still far faster than trade across them, this gave such a naval power the foundations of a massive trade-based empire.

The first steamship was registered in the UK in 1814[9]. By 1850, 1,187 British steamships had been registered; rising to 7,208 in 1900. Over the same period, the number of registered sailing ships declined from 21,449 to 10,773. More importantly, tonnage rose over the period from 2,415,000 to 9,304,000 as fewer steamships were able to move much larger cargoes.

The need to defend this trade fleet had a big impact on the British Royal Navy, which grew dramatically between 1800 and the end of the war in 1918. The navy of 1800 comprised 127 battleships and 158 cruisers, while the navy in 1918 comprised 70 battleships, 143 cruisers, 443 destroyers and frigates, and 147 submarines.

The growth of the Royal Navy – which was to reach its zenith in 1945 – obscures a fundamental contradiction at the heart of imperialism. While coal enabled the expansion of trade – and of the fleets to defend it – on a truly global scale, it was the ongoing availability of coal which determined the winners and losers. As Steven Gray explains[10]:

"More than ever, ships relied on infrastructure – particularly coaling facilities – without which even a fleet as large and powerful as Britain's would be rendered impotent. Yet it is too simplistic to see the movement of steamships as dependent on a static network of coaling stations. Fuel did not simply appear at stations across

the globe, but was subject to multiple movements before arriving. It needed to be sourced, moved to ports, shipped, and unloaded. There is, therefore, a need to recognise that ships relied on the separate flows and networks of fuel."

In the course of the nineteenth century, Britain needed to develop mining and transportation infrastructure around the world. The imperialist nature of this was that for the period in which Britain led the world in steam technologies – roughly 1815 to 1860 – the various nations whose infrastructure was being developed were obliged to borrow in pounds sterling to fund it. After 1860, the law of combined and uneven development eroded Britain's dominance, as Germany and the USA were able to adopt leading edge technologies while Britain remained invested in the technologies of an earlier period.

Between the mid-fifteenth and mid-nineteenth centuries the development of ocean-going shipping meant that it was quicker and easier to sail around continents than it was to travel across them on land. From the mid-nineteenth century, however, the network of railways initially designed to transport resources – including fuel – to the ports had the unwanted (by the naval empires) side effect of opening up entire continents. In Europe, Germany – whose access to the sea was limited – eclipsed Britain's industry, while the USA outpaced both. Even supposedly backward Russia – aided by French investment – developed a sizable railway network in the first decade of the twentieth century; a causal factor in the outbreak of war in August 1914.

War, too, was transformed by coal. In the long era of renewable energy, war casualties were surprisingly low. The Hundred Years War between England and France between 1337 and 1453 resulted in some 2.8 million deaths. Britain's bloodiest battle – Towton in 1461 – resulted in around 28,000 deaths, while the Wars of the Roses between 1455 and 1485 accounted for around 50,000 deaths. The American War of Independence killed around 120,000 people, the American Civil War – arguably the first industrialised war (and a harbinger of things to come) around 800,000. The First World War took industrialised slaughter to a new height of 13,500,000 dead; nearly three times the death rate of the Napoleonic Wars. Even this, though, was to be eclipsed between 1939 and 1945 after a new energy revolution took the death toll (including civilians, who became a deliberate target of war for the first time) to 85,000,000.

Just as coal was initially regarded as inferior to charcoal, the potential of oil as a fuel was initially disregarded. It was the decimation of the Atlantic whale population in the early nineteenth century which was to drive the initial development of American oil fields in Pennsylvania and Oklahoma. Whale oil had been the main fuel for lighting and was an important lubricant for transport and manufacturing machinery. With the whale population in serious decline by the late 1850s, demand for kerosene – a by-product of oil – began to increase. Initially, both diesel and petrol were regarded as waste products. However, with the price of both at rock bottom, existing patents for gas and liquid powered internal combustion engines were dusted off. In 1864, Nikolaus Otto had patented the first atmospheric gas engine. In 1872, American George Brayton invented the first commercial liquid-fuelled internal combustion engine. In 1886, Karl Benz began the first commercial production of motor vehicles with the internal combustion engine. Rudolf Diesel patented the first – and far more powerful – diesel engines in the 1890s. These technologies, though, were in an embryonic state when war broke out in August 1914.

It was the interwar period in the USA, and the post-1945 period in the rest of the world, when the switch from coal to oil was completed. And over the twentieth century, the USA did to Britain (and the rest of the world) what Britain had done in the nineteenth. The suite of technologies that accompanied oil was superior in every way to the coal technologies of the steam age. Transport could carry more goods at less cost. An entirely new form of air transport gradually reduced the time needed to cross continents and oceans. Journeys which, even in the fastest steam ships, used to take weeks could be completed in less than two days; and in the *Concorde* the journey between New York and London could be completed in just three hours.

Although the difference in energy density between coal and oil is small – 25-35 mejajoules per kilogram compared to 45 megajoules per kilogram for diesel – the impact on global trade of the industrial switch from coal to oil was enormous. As historian Paul Kennedy explains[11]:

"The accumulated world industrial output between 1953 and 1973 was comparable in volume to that of the entire century and a half which separated 1953 from 1800. The recovery of war-damaged economies, the development of new technologies, the continued shift from agriculture to industry, the harnessing of national resources within 'planned economies,' and the spread of industrialization to

the Third World all helped to effect this dramatic change. In an even more emphatic way, and for much the same reasons, the volume of world trade also grew spectacularly after 1945..."

American technology and the American dollar underwrote the transition, allowing the USA to emerge as the world's leading power in the post-war years. But the USA encountered the same fuel-network problem as the British a century before. To protect the global oil-based trade network required an oil-powered combined arms military which, in turn required the massive network of American military bases which sprang up during the Cold War. To maintain this network required that the world's oil resources be opened up. This meant that the infrastructure of states with oil resources be developed and maintained. The tendency – "the curse of oil" – for undemocratic local elites to keep the proceeds of oil for themselves while inflicting all of the exploitation and pollution on their people regularly resulted in revolt and revolution; with the USA military – often at large cost to itself – routinely supporting the forces of oppression against the forces of democracy.

As with coal, oil is a finite resource – the faster it is extracted, the quicker it will deplete. In 1956, a Shell geologist Marion King Hubbert calculated that there is a delay of roughly 40 years between the discovery of an oil deposit and its peak extraction. Since the biggest US deposits had been discovered by the early 1930s, Hubbert calculated that *US* peak oil extraction would occur in 1970. Hubbert was correct – although not for strictly geological reasons. Peak extraction of *conventional* oil in the USA was in 1971. But the reason for this was economic – there was still plenty of cheaper conventional oil – much of it extracted by American companies – elsewhere in the world. It was only when the price of oil increased following the oil shocks of the 1970s that more expensive deposits in Alaska and the Gulf of Mexico became viable. Indeed, following the even bigger oil shocks either side of the 2008 financial crash, US *unconventional* oil extraction passed the 1971 peak; with a new peak reached in 2018.

Unfortunately, almost all of the economic theory and modelling taught in schools and universities today is based upon the unique oil based expansion which occurred between 1953 and 1973. Peak US conventional oil extraction, the end of the post-war Bretton Woods monetary system and the first oil shock in 1973 served to plunge the world economy into a crisis which it has mitigated – but never resolved – ever since.

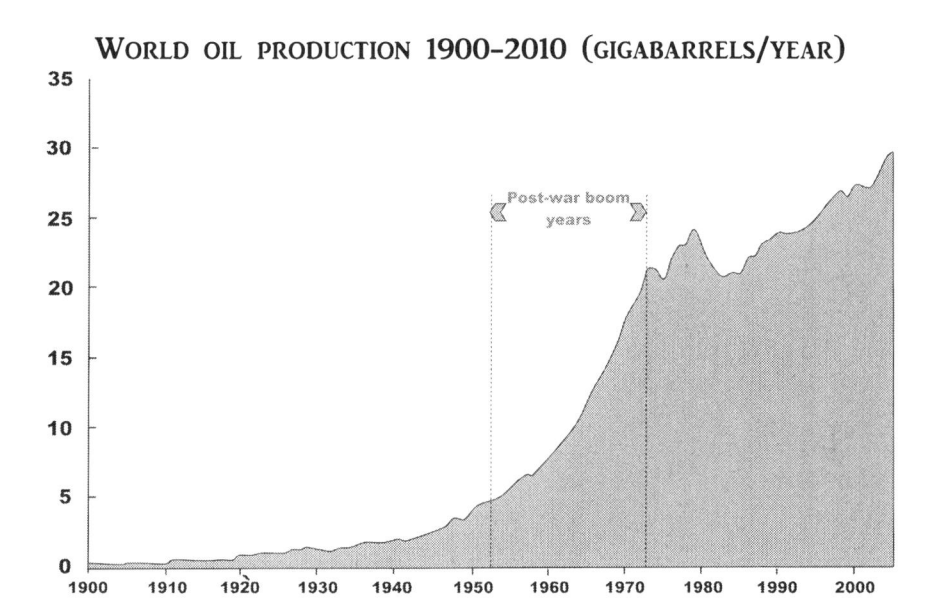

WORLD OIL PRODUCTION 1900–2010 (GIGABARRELS/YEAR)

Notice that we actually produced far more oil in the years following the oil shocks of the 1970s. Volume, however, is not the driving force. The *rate* of energy growth drives the rate of growth in the wider economy. In this way, the massive growth in currency printing in the years after the Second World War – itself an attempt to prevent Western Europe and Japan from falling into the Soviet sphere of influence during the Cold War – drew forth sufficient energy to power a boom that allowed ordinary working people to experience a huge improvement in their standard of living compared to the standards of the 1930s.

The inflation of the 1970s has been blamed on everything from militant unions, price-gouging bosses and improvident governments. The underlying cause, though, was that once the energy available to the economy ceased growing exponentially, the exponential growth in currency printing could only result in the devaluation of the currency itself. This always appears to the lay person as increasing prices; in reality, it is that each new dollar, pound or yen printed into circulation steals a fraction of the value of the currency already in circulation.

The oil shock in 1973 was the first occasion in the post-war years that the economy was faced with a supply-side crisis. Up to that point, economic slowdowns were the result of a fall in *demand* – the amount of purchasing power in the economy – which could be offset by government currency printing. In a supply-side crisis, however, the usual practice of printing currency to spend on increased pensions, benefits and public sector wages, together with investment in public works, could not restore global oil supplies to surplus. Instead, the new currency served only to drive up the price of oil, of commodities produced with oil, and goods transported using oil.

The first oil shock had been partially artificial. Prior to 1971, the land-based US oil industry – via the Texas Railroad Commission (TRC) cartel – had fixed the global price of oil. In the event that prices began to rise, the TRC would order an increase in output. In the event that prices fell, the TRC would order a cut in production. In this way, prices stayed around $20-25 (in today's dollars) – enough to provide the industry with a profit while allowing the broader economy to grow. The problem was that oil extraction in the Middle East and North Africa was more expensive than the in the USA; so that their profits and surplus energy for their domestic economies was lower than in the USA. When – in 1971 – US oil extraction peaked, the TRC lost its monopoly and a new embryonic cartel – OPEC – began to flex its muscles.

USA and European support for Israel in the 1973 war provided the pretext for an OPEC oil embargo which would have arrived in some form anyway. Its result was devastating for economies which had only recently made the switch from coal to oil. Images of long queues for rationed petrol provide the most enduring memories of the crisis; but the real sting was the fall in supplies of diesel to transport, agriculture and critical industry. And as shortage translated into inflation, the crisis morphed into an industrial and political conflict.

Fear of fascism and communism had driven the political consensus which emerged out of the ashes of World War Two. Since both forms of extremism were believed to be the consequence of the unemployment and collapse in living standards in the 1930s, governments committed themselves to maintaining full-employment at all costs. In part this was achieved through public investment in infrastructure and in various forms of nationalised industries. In part it was achieved by maintaining a social safety net of pensions and benefits at a level which prevented unemployed, sick, disabled or old people from falling into poverty.

The downside of this was that trade unions – especially in critical infrastructure like mines, docks, railways, steel and power – had far greater bargaining power than could have been dreamed of in the pre-war years. The industrial trade-off that was maintained during the boom years prior to 1973 was that organised labour would trade productivity for pay. That is, by agreeing to changes in work practices which expanded output for the same or lower inputs, organised labour would receive the bigger share of the profits gained.

This was already causing problems by the late 1960s as demand for increased pay continued even as productivity gains slowed. The UK Labour Party's 1969 White Paper, *In Place of Strife*[12], was an attempt to create a corporate tripartite structure between the state, capital and unions similar to that developed in West Germany and Japan. However, Labour lost the 1970 election to a Tory government initially wedded to the approach known today as neoliberalism. The Heath government sought to deregulate capital while imposing new restrictions upon organised labour – through measures such as the 1971 Industrial Relations Act – to change the industrial balance of power in favour of capital.

Heath, though, was thwarted as much by a Tory party still wedded to the post-war settlement as by the series of strikes and disputes that ended the Industrial Relations Act and ultimately led to Heath calling and losing the February 1974 general election[†].

Labour's return to government did little to alter the economic crisis that Britain was caught in. The combination of US peak oil extraction and Nixon reneging on the post-war pledge to maintain the US dollar at a rate of $35 to an ounce of gold had resulted in the USA's inflation – caused by deficit spending on the Vietnam and Cold Wars – being re-exported to Western Europe. A British economy which had insisted on maintaining its military and the remnants of its empire instead of rebuilding its economy in the aftermath of World War Two was particularly badly hit. Inflation shot into double figures even as a handful of powerful ("aristocracy of labour") trade unions won pay increases well in excess of the five percent formally agreed with the Labour government. By February 1975, Heath was relegated to the backbenches; where he sat sullenly for the rest of his days. In his place was a leader who was even considered to be an extremist by members of her own front bench. Nevertheless, Margaret Thatcher's brand of

---

† Heath actually won the popular vote, but held fewer seats than the Labour opposition, which went on to form a minority government.

neoliberalism, which put sound money and conquering inflation ahead of full-employment, struck a chord with a baby boomer generation which had no memory of the Great Depression or the war.

The political drama culminated in the 1978/79 "winter of discontent," which saw those workers who had not been part of the aristocracy of labour and who had not enjoyed even the five percent pay increase agreed by government taking to the streets. Grave diggers, refuse collectors, an army of public sector clerical workers, shop workers and bakers all downed tools; providing the media with the photographs of refuse mountains and unburied coffins which shaped the image of the crisis. Behind the scenes, however, everything rested upon developments in the North Sea east of Aberdeen.

The Labour government desperately clung onto power through 1978 in the hope that the first barrels of oil from the newly industrialised North Sea fields would make landfall while they were still in office. If it had done so, the recent history of the UK might have been very different. The revenue from the North Sea would provide the government with the income to finally modernise an economy which had fallen well behind its European neighbours and which was fast being overtaken by its Asian competitors. The Tory opposition, in contrast, was determined to use the proceeds from the North Sea to deregulate and further empower Britain's City of London banking and finance sector.

Thatcher won, of course. The baby boomers provided her with the votes she needed to consign the old post war consensus to the dustbin of history. In a matter of months, British industry was decimated; with more than two million jobs lost as the government removed what it considered to be excess currency from circulation. Critical infrastructure such as rail, steel and coal mining was systematically undermined. By the 1980s, these were far weaker than was perceived by many on the political right. Moreover, a series of new industrial laws and regulations which made Heath's Industrial Relations Act look benign, together with a degree of stockpiling, allowed the Thatcher government to provoke and win a series of industrial disputes which effectively ended trade union power in the UK.

The big change in the Thatcher years, however, was almost accidental. The policy which won so many baby boomers to the Tories in 1979 was the promise to sell off Britain's massive stock of council housing. For younger people who, prior to 1979, found themselves excluded (by regulation) from the mortgage market while simultaneously facing shortages of rented accommodation, the promise to sell off public housing (with the broken promise to use the proceeds to build more) was a vote-winner. But making promises is one thing; keeping them is another matter. And one of the reasons why so many British people were living in rented public housing was that they could not access mortgages to purchase private housing.

Regulations introduced to prevent a repeat of the Great Depression had largely excluded banks from issuing mortgages. Instead, most house buyers depended upon mortgages from building societies which operated in a similar way to modern credit unions, and which were usually named after the places they grew up in. These building societies operated in the way even modern economists wrongly believe banks operate – they lent savers' deposits to borrowers in exchange for higher interest than they returned to savers. In 1979, though, the Bank of England imposed strict capital requirements on building societies; thereby preventing them from issuing anything close to the number of mortgages which would be needed for the Thatcher government to achieve its vision of a "home-owning democracy."

The impact of Thatcher's deregulation of the banking sector – which began with the opening up of the mortgage market in 1980 – can be seen in the historical debt to GDP data compiled by Steve Keen:

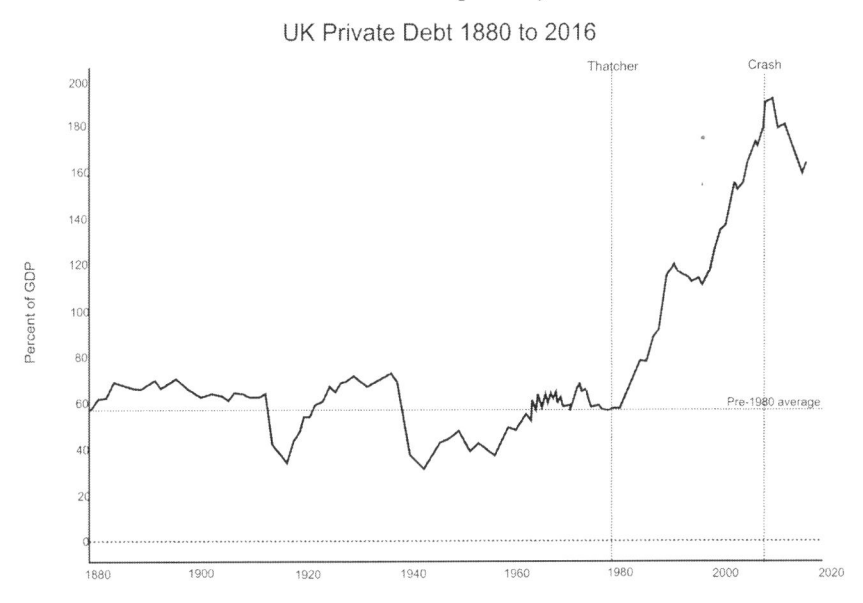

UK Private Debt 1880 to 2016

Whether she knew it or not, from 1980 Thatcher began the process of handing Britain's money supply to the private sector. Banks, you see, are very different creatures to building societies. Whereas a building society needs savers' deposits before it can lend, a bank need only have a special account at the central bank together with a stock of a special currency called "central bank reserves" or "M0 money." With this in place, a bank creates new currency every time it issues a loan. And so, ironically, while the government was busy removing the currency that it creates – mainly notes and coins –from the economy, the banks were beginning to flood the economy with new debt-based currency of their own.

The "Big Bang" reforms in 1986 marked the high point for deregulation; ushering in a feeding frenzy for banks which saw almost all of the UK's building societies bribing their members to allow them to convert to banks. Within a decade, formerly conservative, parochial banks like the Midland, National Westminster and Royal Bank of Scotland became multinational giants pumping out mortgages and credit cards to anyone who wanted them. By the 1990s, with the global economy booming on the back of the new debt-based currency, householders struggled to open their front doors because of the mountain of pre-approved debt offers piling up on their doormats.

In the end, though, all of that debt-based currency depended upon a growing economy within which borrowers could afford to repay their debts with interest. This, in turn, depended upon a steadily growing flow of relatively low-cost oil. Ian Jack, writing in the *Guardian* in 2013 reflects upon the boom years[13]:

> *"I had the idea for the title when I was walking through a London square around the time of the City's deregulatory 'Big Bang' and Peregrine Worsthorne coining the phrase 'bourgeois triumphalism' to describe the brash behaviour of the newly enriched: the boys who wore red braces and swore long and loud in restaurants. Champagne was becoming an unexceptional drink. The miners had been beaten. A little terraced house in an ordinary bit of London would buy 7.5 similar houses in Bradford. In the seven years since 1979, jobs in manufacturing had declined from about seven million to around five million, and more than nine in every 10 of all jobs lost were located north of the diagonal between the Bristol channel and the Wash. And yet it was also true that more people owned more things – tumble dryers and deep freezers – than ever before, and*

that the average household's disposable income in 1985 was more than 10% higher than it had been in the last days of Jim Callaghan's government.

"Social peace had been bought by tax cuts and welfare benefits, and these had been largely enabled by government income from North Sea oil that by the mid-1980s was delivering the Treasury 10% of its revenues. The question was, how long would this bounty last?"

Jack suggested that the UK would continue to be a major oil producer until the 2040s or 2050s. In fact, Britain's North Sea oil and gas fields peaked in 1999 and output had fallen by 60 percent by 2013. Worse still, Britain had become a net importer of oil in 2004 and a net gas importer the following year. Yes, the fields were still producing, and there was more than enough oil and gas beneath the seabed. The problem was that most of it was too expensive to access. A year after Jack's article was published, the world witnessed a massive crash in oil prices which appeared to answer a question which had dogged "peak oil" analysts for more than a decade – would low *supply* cause prices to rise, or would low *demand* cause them to fall?

In the post-2008 depression, there was simply not enough demand to keep oil prices high enough to attract the investment needed to open up the smaller and more difficult UK fields that remain unexploited. Worse still, at the lower prices, concerns have grown that there is not enough *accessible* oil and gas to cover the cost of decommissioning. Writing in the *Financial Times* in 2016, Kiran Stacey and Alan Livsey reported that[14]:

"Between now and the mid-2050s, around 470 platforms, 5,000 wells, 10,000km of pipelines and 40,000 concrete blocks will have to be removed from the North Sea.

"Decommissioning takes place regularly in other mature basins such as the Gulf of Mexico but nowhere in the oil industry will such a major clean-up have happened in such a short time...

"The industry has always known that it would have to decommission ageing platforms, but the process has been accelerated by an oil price that has crashed from $115 in the summer of 2014 to around $50. This has left half of the operators

in the North Sea — the most expensive place in the world to drill for oil — running at a loss, according to figures from Company Watch, which monitors corporate financial risk.

"These companies face a difficult decision: should they continue to produce oil and gas at a loss, hoping to make the money back if and when the price rebounds or do they pack up altogether, incurring millions of pounds of decommissioning costs in the process? It is prohibitively expensive to come back and start drilling once a well has been left, so any decision to leave is final."

Despite pursuing similar economic policies to Thatcher's, David Cameron and George Osborne failed to repeat the debt-based boom. For almost all of the UK population outside London and a handful of top-tier university towns, living standards declined for the decade after 2008. The reason was not just that the oil which had underwritten Thatcher's debt had dried up; but that global reserves of conventional (i.e. cheap and relatively easy) oil had also peaked. Indeed, the chain of events which led to the 2008 crash and the depression which followed began with peak conventional oil extraction in 2005.

As had happened in 1973, a shortage of oil was followed by a big spike in oil prices. As in 1973, this translated into price increases in goods and services which depended upon oil either for energy, as a material or for transport. According to the economic textbooks, the way to combat this "inflation" was to raise interest rates in order to remove debt-based currency from the economy.

The error in this approach was that the generalised price increases which followed the rise in oil prices from 2005 were not in themselves inflationary. Rather, they were evidence of an economy adjusting itself to the new normal. So long as the supply of currency remained constant, people paying more for oil and oil-related goods and services would translate into people buying less elsewhere in the economy. Without central bank interference, the economy would have settled in a matter of months. Instead, the central bank intervention achieved its aim in the most catastrophic way imaginable.

Although the establishment media were to make a big deal about "sub-prime" borrowers, in many ways these were the victims of the whole sorry saga. At the height of the boom, with property prices rising remorselessly, a shortage of reasonably-priced rental accommodation more or less drove people into the arms of a banking sector which made its profits from issuing loans. For many, the cost of mortgage repayments proved to be less than the monthly rent on someone else's property. And at least with a mortgage you got to own the house at the end of the term. At the very least, you got to sell one house in exchange for the deposit on the next one. So long as the economy continued to boom, and so long as the banks continued to offer low-interest mortgages, sub-prime borrowing was not a problem.

When interest rates rose from 2006, borrowers who had previously been getting by were plunged into arrears. In the USA, borrowers posted the keys to their former homes back to the mortgage company. In the UK, bankruptcies began to rise. In theory, the mortgaged property was an asset of the bank. But once the number of defaults grew, these properties became a liability – nominally worth a lot but in reality unsellable in a market where people were suddenly reluctant to take on new debt.

To protect themselves, banks had securitised the income from their mortgages and sold these on as Securitised Investment Vehicles (SIVs) which had generated enormous profits for the banks during the boom. But as the monthly repayment income ceased, so the SIVs began to fail. To hedge against this, the banks had taken out insurance in the so-called "shadow banking" (i.e. unregulated) sector. As with all insurance, though, these policies had been designed to deal with normal rates of default, not a wholesale collapse in the mortgage sector. And so the insurance also failed.

The big lie was that the banks had a "liquidity crisis" – that they had valuable assets, they just needed time to liquidate (i.e. sell) them. It was on the basis of this lie that banks persuaded governments to use future taxpayers' money to bail out the banks. In reality, the banks had an "insolvency crisis" – they were sat on top of a mountain of worthless paper which had nothing of real substance to back it up. Had governments realised this – and had they been operating in the public interest – they would have allowed the banks to go bust. They could then have nationalised their assets and used the state's ability to create currency to recapitalise them. Instead, states and central banks transferred the bad debt to the public accounts.

In and of itself, this need not have been a problem. Many times in the past, governments have borrowed against the future to escape an immediate crisis. British tax payers, for example, are still paying off loans taken out to fight the Napoleonic Wars and the First World War – the Second World War debt was paid off by 2010. Similar long-term borrowing might have been used to repay the bank bailouts. It was an ideological decision to impose austerity cuts and increase taxes in an attempt to shorten the repayment period. It may, however, have inadvertently delayed an even bigger crisis.

The underlying and usually unchallenged assumption in economics (and the politics derived from it) is that economic growth is a constant. For the best part of three centuries, growth has been the norm – only temporarily interrupted by short periods of recession. Moreover, with most economic textbooks written by economists who grew up in the boom years 1953-73, high levels of growth are treated as normal despite their being abnormal even to industrial civilisation. Growth, however, depends upon energy – either an absolute increase in fuel extraction or via productivity gains derived from the more efficient use of energy. Spectacular growth in the years after World War Two was achieved by both. Later – and more modest – achievements came primarily from productivity gains that inevitably involve diminishing returns.

In the event that the currency created to bail out the banks in 2008 had leaked out into the wider economy in the following years, we would have experienced crippling inflation rather than a new round of economic growth. This is simply because the world no longer has access to the fuel supplies required to generate a new round of growth.

To be clear here, this is an *energy* issue, not a financial one. It takes energy to obtain energy, and as the energy cost of obtaining energy increases, so the energy available to the wider economy decreases.

By 2008, the world economy had reached the beginning of the "net energy cliff" – the point at which the average number of energy units obtained for each unit expended reached 20:1. At this point, simply maintaining the physical infrastructure – bridges, railways, roads, ports, etc. – that we have already created is a struggle. Further growth is all but beyond us. And beyond this point we face a rapid decent into a future in which almost all of today's energy must be used to obtain energy for tomorrow.

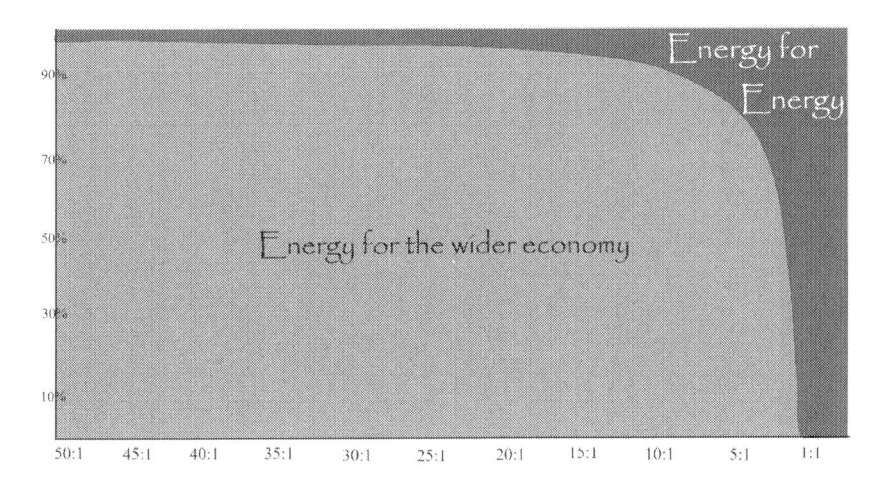

[Chart: Y-axis labeled 10% to 90%; X-axis from 50:1 to 1:1. Two regions labeled "Energy for the wider economy" and "Energy for Energy".]

This, though, is obscured by localised quirks in the interaction between finance and energy. In order to bail out the wider financial sector after 2008, central banks had to lower interest rates close to zero. This allowed so-called "zombie" businesses and households to continue servicing debts that they would never be able to repay. At the same time, they hoped that the low cost of currency would translate into more borrowing both to restart the mortgage sector and to kick-start businesses. The downside, however, was that savers and institutional investors struggled to get an adequate return.

The result was a "search for yield" which resulted in rising demand for so-called "junk bonds" – the high risk bonds issued by companies which couldn't get finance from the banks. One beneficiary of this was the US hydraulic fracturing industry which was to spend billions of dollars extracting millions of dollars' worth of oil and gas over the following decade. Like all of the other zombies, so long as the wells kept pumping and the oil price stayed above $50 per barrel, the frackers could service their debts despite having zero chance of ever repaying them. Meanwhile, junk bond investors were happy to turn a blind eye so long as the monthly interest payments continued to flow.

US hydraulically fractured oil accounts for *all* of the global rise in oil extraction between 2008 and 2018 – the year that global oil extraction finally peaked. No month between November 2018 and December 2019 was to see oil extraction pass the peak of November 2018. And with the crash in global demand resulting from the response to the Covid-19 pandemic, it is unlikely that oil extraction will ever get close to that figure again.

In this way, financialisation is the mechanism through which energy is moved out of the shrinking non-energy sectors of the economy in order to extract new fuel sources that would otherwise be unaffordable. Nor does the search for yield limit itself to oil. Internationally, it has aided a massive increase in the use of fossil fuels of all kinds.

Ironically, it was the return to an older fossil fuel – coal – in China and India in the years after 2008 which provided the global economy with just enough economic activity to prevent a complete collapse. But even before Covid-19 shut down China's industrial regions, growth had begun to slow in response to falling demand in the developed western economies. The dream of a Chinese working class with sufficient purchasing power to allow China to escape the constraints of the global economy was never realised. As the western economies run out of power, China is doomed to follow.

Unlike the early twentieth century there is no obvious replacement for oil waiting in the wings in the twenty-first. A great deal of hope had been put in nuclear energy because of the vast difference in potential energy released by breaking the bonds in the nucleus compared to breaking electron (chemical) bonds. Whereas the energy density of diesel is around 45MJ/Kg the energy density of uranium in a breeder reactor is around 86,000 MJ/Kg. The problem, however, is that nobody has figured out how to release nuclear energy in a useable and *economically* viable manner. The various – essentially steam technology – pressurised water reactors dotted around the planet are the nuclear equivalent of Trevithick's steam engine or the *Wright Flyer*. Clearly, if a similar process of productivity gains to those seen with coal and oil technologies were to occur, the suite of technologies and the ensuing growth in economic activities would be as incomprehensible to us today as our technology would have been to a resident of eighteenth century England. For now, though, nobody knows how to utilise nuclear energy. The cost of building the power stations – each of which is unique – far outweighs the energy generated. Thus, even though the uranium fuel is both cheap and relatively abundant, the inability to use it efficiently all but rules out nuclear as a new energy revolution[†].

[†] The holy grail of nuclear fusion has been "twenty years away" for at least 60 years. Meanwhile, modular – i.e. mass produced – molten salt and molten metal reactors have yet to progress beyond the experimental stage.

Renewable energy – humanity's power source for the 250,000 years or so *prior to* industrialisation – is a non-starter on energy density grounds. That is, while it is true that more solar energy reaches the Earth in a week than *all of* the fossil fuel energy humans have burned in the past 300 years, we can only harvest a tiny fraction of it – roughly four percent of our total energy consumption. Moreover, while the energy is for all practical purposes renewable, the technologies ought more correctly to be referred to as "non-renewable renewable energy-harvesting technologies." That is, wind turbines and solar panels cannot be manufactured without the heat generated by fossil fuels, and are constructed in part from materials derived from fossil fuels. Nor can they be transported, erected and maintained other than with the use of fossil fuelled vehicles and machinery for which there is no electric alternative.

Hydrogen has a far higher energy density than oil, at around 140MJ/Kg. But although it is the most abundant element in the universe, hydrogen only occurs as part of compounds in nature. This means that a great deal of energy has to be expended to produce hydrogen, making it far more expensive than fuels derived from oil. This is particularly true for the electrolysis process of splitting water into hydrogen and oxygen. Most of the hydrogen currently used in industry is the product of the cheaper process of refining it from natural gas. Hydrogen has two other serious drawbacks. First, it is highly explosive even compared to petrol; so that production and storage require expensive additional safety systems. Second, because it is the smallest atom, leakage is inevitable. Taken together, these problems make a hydrogen-powered vehicle potentially one of the least safe places to be.

With fossil fuel extraction in decline – both in terms of the volume extracted *and* the net energy return – the immediate crisis for humans on planet Earth is that we face a looming energy crunch which *must* result in a decline in overall economic activity. Nor does this only impact the energy sectors of the economy. Global mineral supplies are also threatened by net energy shortages, despite there being more than enough resources beneath the ground. With infinite energy, we could, for example, suck all of the minerals we need out of sea water. But without infinite energy we are stuck with traditional forms of mining and refining which are struggling with declining ore grades in which increasing energy has to be used to offset increasing waste rock.

Last year, scientists at the UK Natural History Museum issued a resources warning to ministers who mistakenly believe we can switch from fossil fuels to renewable electricity[15]:

> *"To replace all UK-based vehicles today with electric vehicles (not including the LGV and HGV fleets), assuming they use the most resource-frugal next-generation NMC 811 batteries, would take 207,900 tonnes cobalt, 264,600 tonnes of lithium carbonate (LCE), at least 7,200 tonnes of neodymium and dysprosium, in addition to 2,362,500 tonnes copper. This represents, just under two times the total annual world cobalt production, nearly the entire world production of neodymium, three quarters the world's lithium production and at least half of the world's copper production during 2018. Even ensuring the annual supply of electric vehicles only, from 2035 as pledged, will require the UK to annually import the equivalent of the entire annual cobalt needs of European industry.*
>
> *"The worldwide impact: If this analysis is extrapolated to the currently projected estimate of two billion cars worldwide, based on 2018 figures, annual production would have to increase for neodymium and dysprosium by 70%, copper output would need to more than double and cobalt output would need to increase at least three and a half times for the entire period from now until 2050 to satisfy the demand.*
>
> *"Energy cost of metal production: This choice of vehicle comes with an energy cost too. Energy costs for cobalt production are estimated at 7000-8000 kWh for every tonne of metal produced and for copper 9000 kWh/t. The rare-earth energy costs are at least 3350 kWh/t, so for the target of all 31.5 million cars that requires 22.5 TWh of power to produce the new metals for the UK fleet, amounting to 6% of the UK's current annual electrical usage. Extrapolated to 2 billion cars worldwide, the energy demand for extracting and processing the metals is almost 4 times the total annual UK electrical output."*

The envisaged low-carbon future is now beyond us. With insufficient energy, we cannot produce the minerals required; and without the minerals there can be no transformation beyond a handful of local and regional pockets dotted across the developed states. The only real question remaining to be answered is which activities we will – collectively – opt to maintain and which we will let go. Energy, of course and despite the demands of environmentalists, will be non-negotiable since without *any* of our current energy sources the collapse will be far worse. Some public services such as healthcare and education may also receive a disproportionate amount of the energy that remains to the non-energy sectors of the economy. But that merely means that other sectors such as media, arts and tech are likely to be more readily ditched, de-layered and simplified.

Exactly how this will play out is anyone's guess. Nobody writing immediately after the 2008 crash would have foreseen the decade of – albeit anaemic – growth which followed. The idea that the USA – whose oil production had been in decline since 1971 – would emerge as the world's largest oil extractor would have been dismissed as insanity. Nevertheless, that is the decade that we have just lived through. In the absence of a new *energy-dense* power source, however, it will have been the last decade during which industrialised economic growth was possible. Shrinking net energy means a shrinking economy. The only question that remains is how, exactly, that shrinkage occurs. As always, there will be winners and losers.

REFERENCES

[1] Ponting, c. 2001. *World History: A New Perspective.* Pimlico

[2] Hersh, Jonathan and Voth, Hans-Joachim, Sweet Diversity: Colonial Goods and the Rise of European Living Standards after 1492 (July 17, 2009). Available at SSRN: https://ssrn.com/abstract=1402322

[3] "The Enlightenment: Psychoactive Globalisation" https://evolutionofdruguse.wordpress.com/biology-driver/from-depressant-to-stimulant-the-enlightenment

[4] *A History of the World in 6 Glasses.* 2006. Walker Publishing Company.

[5] Mitchell, B.R. 1988. *British Historical Statistics.* P247.

[6] Department for Business, Energy and Industrial Strategy. 2013 (updated 2019). *Historical coal data: coal production, availability and consumption 1853 to 2018.* www.gov.uk/government/statistical-data-sets/historical-coal-data-coal-production-availability-and-consumption

[7] "The development of the railway network in Britain 1825-1911." Cambridge e-Resources for teaching economic history and historical economic geography: www.campop.geog.cam.ac.uk/research/projects/transport/onlineatlas/railways.pdf

[8] Ibid

[9] Mitchell, R.B. Ibid.

[10] "Fuelling mobility: coal and Britain's naval power, c. 1870–1914." University of Portsmouth.
https://researchportal.port.ac.uk/portal/files/7282023/Fuelling_mobility.pdf

[11] Kennedy, P. 2017. The Rise and Fall of the Great Powers: Economic Change and Military Conflict from 1500-2000. William Collins; New Ed edition.

[12] www.nationalarchives.gov.uk/cabinetpapers/themes/industrial-unrest.htm

[13] "North Sea oil fuelled the 80s boom, but it was, and remains, strangely invisible" *Guardian*. 19 April 2013. www.theguardian.com/commentisfree/2013/apr/19/north-sea-oil-80s-boom

[14] "North Sea oil: The £30bn break-up" *Financial Times*. 8 June 2016. www.ft.com/content/b3255c92-2bca-11e6-a18d-a96ab29e3c95

[15] "Leading scientists set out resource challenge of meeting net zero emissions in the UK by 2050" *Natural History Museum*. 5 June 2019. www.nhm.ac.uk/press-office/press-releases/leading-scientists-set-out-resource-challenge-of-meeting-net-zer.html

Getting the Economy Wrong

(1): The Financial and the Real

For most people, "the economy" is some strange place entirely separate from their day-to-day lives. Rather like some ancient religion, it has a language of its own and a priesthood of economists, treasury officials, central bankers and specialist journalists to guide us mere mortals. We – sort of – understand that decisions taken about this thing called "the economy" have an effect on our lives; but the exact mechanisms remain a mystery. We know that tax policy has a big impact on our standard of living. We also understand that the decision to lower or raise interest rates determines how much of our income goes on debt repayments. But the exact mechanisms remain a mystery; as do the linkages between the two.

The fact that "the economy" is shrouded in fog is no accident. Nor is it a measure of any lack of intelligence on our part. Rather, it is the consequence of a deliberate effort – honed over centuries – to ensure that the governed *never* understand how elites maintain their wealth and power. Language – originally developed so that we might share knowledge and insight – is usurped by the financiers and the economists to mystify and obfuscate; to create an invisible wall between the people and the elites. The language used by those who run "the economy" is the linguistic equivalent of a barbed wire fence and a giant "Keep Out!" Sign.

In any case, most of us are so drained from the rigours of day-to-day life that we have no energy left over to think about economic matters beyond those – wages, utility bills, credit card debts, mortgage repayments, etc. – which are immediate. As in so many areas of life, we are obliged to trust that clever people somewhere else know what they are doing. Unfortunately, when it comes to the economy, what "they" are doing amounts to the organised cover up of wholesale theft.

The economy, you see, is not what they want you to believe. It is not primarily about treasury departments, central banks and university economics departments. The economy is really the sum total of *everything* that humans do. Consider the mundane. The bed that you awoke in this morning is the end product of a network of supply chains which stretch around the planet. The metal in the springs was mined in a different country before being shipped to a steelworks and then on to a wire mill. The cotton in the fabric was grown in a different part of the world before being shipped to a mill for weaving into fabric. The mattress was assembled in yet another country; and the bed frame in another country again. The shampoo, body wash and toothpaste which you used were made using oil drilled from a well in the Middle East which was transported to a chemical plant before being shipped on to the detergent factory which added the colour and scent before sending it on to the wholesaler. The clothes you put on were made on the other side of the planet from a range of natural and synthetic materials which were also shipped halfway around the world. The breakfast cereal which you ate was grown on another continent. The car that you drove to work in is made of tens of thousands of individual components manufactured in different factories around the world before being shipped to your nearest assembly plant. The number of individual workers involved just in getting you to work in the morning is truly mind boggling. Add together all of the economic transactions involved and we find it runs to billions.

We take all of this for granted. The only relationship that we have within this intricate web of the *real* economy is with the retailer who sold us the end product. Take the time to read the label and we might find the country of origin – although even this may refer only to the country where something was assembled rather than the several countries where individual components were made or where raw resources were grown or mined. Insofar as most of us think about where something "came from," we think only of the shop where we bought it.

We should not be ashamed of this. The odds are that the purchasing manager for the shop where we bought the item is also unaware of its origin. They know only the wholesaler who supplied it. The wholesaler, in turn, knows only the shipping agent who only knows the export company, which only knows the assembly plant, which only knows the component factories, who only know the wholesalers of their component parts, etc. practically ad infinitum.

There is no beginning or end to this real economy. Rather it is the intricate dance which every human who ever lived has participated in throughout their lives. Each seeking to improve their condition or prevent its deterioration, but thereby impacting upon the lives of those around them. Sometimes cooperating, sometimes coercing; but always with unintended consequences. The development of the oil industry is a case in point, since the quest to drill for oil was for an entirely different purpose to the uses oil is put to today.

Industrialisation and a growing population drove North American whalers to rapidly deplete Atlantic whale populations. So much so that the uses to which whales products were put – beyond food – were undermined. Whale fat, for example, was used as a lubricant to minimise damage to cart wheels. The most widespread use of whale oil, though, was as lamp fuel. As whale oil shortages became endemic, prices rose so high that people looked for alternatives. And one relatively cheap alternative was kerosene – a product of refined oil.

Carriage building in the USA grew up on the western shore of Lake Erie at the point where cargo ships which had sailed through the St Lawrence waterway and through the great lakes landed their cargoes to be transported by land and river into the continental USA. It made sense to build carriages where they were needed rather than having to transport the carriages from elsewhere. Those carriage makers had used whale oil as a lubricant, and now turned to oil as an alternative. It was, though, a waste product from the kerosene industry which was to put that region of the USA on the international map.

Gasoline (petrol) began as an unwanted waste product looking for a use. And because it is a gas (vapour) at room temperature, one potential use was as a fuel for the various gas internal combustion engines which had been patented long before. Prior to the production of large volumes of gasoline, explosive gases were either too expensive or too volatile to allow internal combustion engines to be more than an engineering curiosity. Gasoline, however, proved just volatile enough to provide motive power without damaging the engine materials. And with oil coming out of the ground in abundance, it was cheap enough to make the production of motorised carriages – or "cars" – worthwhile. Furthermore, since it made no sense to create an entirely new motorised carriage industry, the existing carriage makers in Detroit simply incorporated internal combustion engine plants into their factories; and the "motor city" was born.

The point is that nobody involved in the supply of whale oil as a lighting fuel set out to create the oil industry, to produce cars or indeed to pollute the biosphere to the point of near collapse... it just happened. Each person in the chain just doing what made sense to them as they interacted with others around them. And yet the collective and unforeseen consequence was truly Earth-changing.

Make no mistake, this complex web of individual economic transactions which continues day-in/day-out is as crucial to each of our survival as hunting and gathering was to our distant ancestors. Each of us fulfilling our niche within the system is what guarantees that food, clothing, shelter, transportation, clean water, fuel and electricity are available when we need them. Disrupt the whole in minor ways and it will reset – in the way that American lighting oil could be switched from whale oil to kerosene. Too large a disruption – like a war or a plague – and the entire system might come tumbling down.

Until recently, though, the single biggest threat to the real economy has come from the banking and financial sector. In the same way as the crash in 1929 caused a worldwide recession which ushered in a period of political extremism, the 2008 crash has caused stagnation, social unrest and a rise of nationalist populist parties which threatens to unravel the current version of the global economy... a process which may undermine those all too essential supply chains.

(2): THE PROBLEM OF MONEY

Most importantly, "the economy" is viewed through the lens of a magical substance which is the nearest thing we have to the religious understanding of divine spirit. As Charles Eisenstein observes[1]:

> *"It is hugely ironic and hugely significant that the one thing on the planet most closely resembling the forgoing conception of the divine is money. It is an invisible, immortal force that surrounds and steers all things, omnipotent and limitless, an 'invisible hand' that, it is said, makes the world go 'round. Yet, money today is an abstraction, at most symbols on a piece of paper but usually mere bits in a computer. It exists in a realm far removed from materiality. In that realm, it is exempt from nature's most important laws, for it does not decay and return to the soil as all other things do, but is rather preserved, changeless, in its vaults and computer files, even growing with time thanks to interest...*
>
> *"Looking down from Olympian heights, the financiers called themselves 'masters of the universe,' channelling the power of the god they served to bring fortune or ruin upon the masses, to literally move mountains, raze forests, change the course of rivers, cause the rise and fall of nations.*

> *"What we call recession, an earlier culture might have called 'God abandoning the world.' Money is disappearing, and with it another property of spirit: the animating force of the human realm. At this writing, all over the world machines stand idle. Factories have ground to a halt; construction equipment sits derelict in the yard; parks and libraries are closing; and millions go homeless and hungry while housing units stand vacant and food rots in the warehouses. Yet all the human and material inputs to build the houses, distribute the food, and run the factories still exist. It is rather something immaterial, that animating spirit, which has fled. What has fled is money. That is the only thing missing, so insubstantial (in the form of electrons in computers) that it can hardly be said to exist at all, yet so powerful that without it, human productivity grinds to a halt."*

And yet, for all of its importance to our lives, money is little understood even among those who occupy positions of power. Among the most worrying revelations to emerge following the 2008 crash was that at no point in an economics degree course were students – the economic policymakers of the future – taught what money is and where it comes from. As economist Steve Keen – one of the few economists who did teach about money – revealed[2]:

> *"It may astonish non-economists to learn that conventionally trained economists ignore the role of credit and private debt in the economy – and frankly, it is astonishing. But it is the truth. Even today, only a handful of the most rebellious of mainstream 'neoclassical' economists – people like Joe Stiglitz and Paul Krugman – pay any attention to the role of private debt in the economy, and even they do so from the perspective of an economic theory in which money and debt play no intrinsic role. An economic theory that ignores the role of money and debt in a market economy cannot possibly make sense of the complex, monetary, credit-based economy in which we live. Yet that is the theory that has dominated economics for the last half-century."*

Our political leaders were equally clueless about money. A 2017 survey of Members of Parliament by the campaign group Positive Money found that a staggering 85 percent of them did not understand where money comes from[3]. Nevertheless, these are the people who every year vote on a Finance Bill (The Budget) which directly affects every household and every business in the land.

Among the biggest frauds committed on the public by the quasi-religion of economics was a story entirely concocted by Adam Smith which has come to be taught as gospel truth ever since. To this day if you ask the man or woman in the street *why* money was invented you will be lucky to find one who does not offer a story about bartering. In my book *The Consciousness of Sheep* I refer to Smith's version of the origins of money as a fairy story[4]:

> *"Try to imagine a world quite different to ours:*
>
> *"We find ourselves in a typical English village in the year 1090. It is market day. The people who work in the fields around the village have come together to trade their wares.*
>
> *"We observe a villager who has a chicken that he wants to exchange for some apples. But there is a problem. The only villager who has apples to exchange is not interested in chickens. Instead, he wants some grain seeds to sow for next year's crop. So our chicken toting villager must try to find someone who is prepared to swap grain seeds for a chicken. But – wouldn't you guess – the person who has grain seeds wants cheese. So our villager sets off to find someone who wants to swap a chicken for some cheese. Unfortunately, the only villager with cheese is looking for flour. So off our villager goes to find someone who has flour to swap. And so it goes on...*
>
> *"It takes our intrepid chicken-swapping villager all day to work out a chain of barter trades that will ultimately result in his coming away with the apples that he wanted.*
>
> *"And if you think that is bad, let us look at the haggling process that has to occur to work out exactly how much cheese, flour, grain seed and apples would make up the equivalent worth or "value" of a chicken. Size wouldn't work because some highly valued goods (such as spices) come in small quantities. Nor would weight, colour, taste, or a whole host of possible measures. In practice, what mattered to people in an eleventh century English village was the time it took to grow, rear or create the item offered for trade together with the skill level required to create it and cost of the fodder, seeds, tools, and raw materials needed for its manufacture. Let us remember too that it is not just our villager who has to undertake this complex process of bartering. Every other villager is doing the*

same thing! Each must calculate a complicated exchange chain to get him from the item that he has to the item that he wants. And at each link in the complicated chain he must spend time haggling with the other person in the trade to get sufficient amounts of the goods on offer to make the next exchange.

"This bartering process is not about the trading of luxury items. This is about obtaining sufficient food to stay alive; especially during the long hard winter months when there is little fresh food to be found. No wonder these early feudal villages struggled to prevent collapse!

"Fortunately one morning a Norman knight rides into the village to save the day. For the knight comes bearing items so radical that they will truly revolutionise the way these villages operate. It is these – almost magical items – that will put these people on a direct historical line, through mercantilism, imperialism and an industrial revolution, to our modern civilisation. The knight comes bearing money! Coins made of a standard weight of precious gold, silver and bronze; coins that bear the image of the king as a stamp of quality and value. From this day forth, the villagers are able to exchange their goods for coins which can, in turn, be used to buy the goods they require. Instead of having to spend the day bartering, they are now free either to produce more goods or to enjoy some recreation.

"This, in essence, is the fairy story that Adam Smith invented to try to explain the origins of money as a basis for his 'Labour Theory of Value'. It is the tale that most economics students are taught. It is a story so deeply embedded in our culture that almost everyone believes it. And, of course, it is complete and utter nonsense!"

There are simply not enough hours in the day for this kind of transacting to occur. Indeed, the notion of value which Smith was attempting to anchor in the workings of a medieval village is not a precursor of money but rather a consequence of its introduction. Most *settled* pre-industrial communities operated on the basis of favour and obligation in a manner which strengthened social bonds. If your neighbour had need of assistance, of food or of some goods that you happened to possess, you were obliged to give it. But woe betides the neighbour who failed to return the favour. The stocks existed to deal with minor lapses while banishment – which meant almost certain death

– awaited those who took without giving in return. Insofar as favours and obligations were counted at all, people used a range of devices including tally sticks and knotted strings to keep record. But none of these could seriously be treated as a measure – still less a store – of value.

Money, though, has been around for as long as humans have kept records. If not used for the routine purchase of goods and services, what was money used for?

To answer this, let me begin with another question. Did you ever wonder why, if the King or Emperor owned the gold and silver mines, he had to raise taxes? Why not simply dig up some more gold and mint some more coins?

The stock answer is that money-printing creates inflation. However, this, once again, is a *consequence* of switching to a cash economy. The true reason in earlier non-cash economies is that there are several itinerant classes of people who cannot integrate their activities into the system of favour and obligation that most people lived within. Merchants, for example, could not wait around for people to provide various favours in exchange for their wares. More importantly – from the King's point of view – soldiers and sailors could neither carry all of the goods – including food – that they needed; nor could they expect villagers to supply it in exchange for some future favour which may never be repaid. Money, then, was the means by which those classes of people who travelled (in an age when the majority of people lived and died within a mile of the place they were born) could pay for the goods and services they needed.

While precious metals have some intrinsic value – in part due to scarcity, in part to density/weight and in part to their chemical properties – they were of little use to people in an economy based on favour and obligation. A gold coin could neither be eaten nor used as fuel for a hearth. To most ordinary people a sack of grain would be far more valuable. Why, then, should ordinary villagers take the money offered as payment by passing soldiers? One reason might be to have money with which to pay for the wares of passing merchants. The more important reason, however, was that the King imposed taxes and it was the job of the soldiers to collect them. Tax gives money a large part of its value because it provides people with the need to engage in cash transactions.

At this point, another *theoretical* property of money comes into play. Money *can be* a store of value. That is, if I sell an item for a gold coin today then I should be able to buy the same item – or something of equivalent value – for the same gold coin in future. But if gold is thought of as "the eternal metal," then cheating might be thought of as the eternal human behaviour.

From the moment the first metal coin was minted, people began to think about ways of counterfeiting. Coins might, for example, be snipped, and the metal shavings collected and melted down. Alternatively, when it was the King who wished to cheat, some base metal could be thrown into the mix before the coins were minted.

While most people perceive the criminality that lies beneath the debasement of currency, few fully understand the nature of the crime. After all, the new coin which has a bit of brass mixed in with the gold looks and feels the same as the pure gold coin. The same is true today of the dollars, pounds and euros printed by the mafia – even the highest trained investigator cannot tell them from the real thing. Where, then, is the crime?

The crime is that prices are a measure of the currency in circulation rather than of the value of the goods and services being bought. The greater the amount of currency in circulation, the higher the price of goods and services will rise. While we have been conditioned to think of this *inflation* in terms of prices increasing – and thus we are encouraged to blame price-gouging businessmen or greedy trade unionists – what is actually happening is that the person or people who debase the currency are stealing a tiny fraction of the *value* of the currency which is already in circulation. Instead of money being a store of value, it is depreciating; so that it is more valuable if it is spent immediately than if it is saved or invested. It matters not a jot whether the counterfeiting is done by gangsters or governments; the effect on everyone who trades in cash is the same.

There are, of course, more obvious crimes that can be committed against people who buy and sell using gold and silver coins. Plain theft is far easier than counterfeiting to commit. History is littered with tales of outlaw bands robbing money and valuables from unwary travellers. Banks initially developed as a safe storage for money and valuables. And as transport systems and communications developed, so it became easier for travellers to move from town to town without needing to carry money with them. Instead, the bank where they deposited their money and valuables could issue them with a receipt – a bank note – which would be accepted by the branch of the bank in the town they were visiting. In this way, a wealthy traveller could – for a small fee – avoid physically moving money. Instead, all of the money on deposit in all of the banks would be exchangeable for banknotes. Indeed, as time went on these banknotes came to be treated as being as good as the gold they represented; and so people began to trade goods and services for banknotes without needing to obtain gold from the bank.

Remember, though, that cheating is in our nature. It wasn't long before someone figured out that the bank always had more money in the vault than its customers needed. Banks could print more banknotes than they had gold to back them with. This would be particularly useful when people wanted to borrow money from the bank. Instead of lending actual gold, the bank could simply print off some banknotes. And so long as people were happy to leave their physical gold in the vault, nobody would ever find out.

Inflation, though, destroys people's faith in currency. As ever more banknotes flooded the system, so prices rose. Eventually the depositors began to ask for their gold back. This resulted in a run on the bank, as queues developed and the bankers realised there was not enough gold in the vaults.

In those days a stout rope was used to remind bankers of their social obligations and to serve as a warning to any future bank official who might be tempted to make loans in excess of the money held in the vault. These days, unfortunately, such actions are rewarded by governments and central banks. Nevertheless, officially such practices have been outlawed by statutes such as Britain's Bank Charter Act of 1844 which forbids anyone other than the Crown to create money. Sadly, the 1844 Act could only outlaw the coins and notes which constituted the money of the day; so that while it was clearly the intention of Parliament to ban bank counterfeiting, by using more modern financial vehicles such as cheque accounts and securitised loans, modern banks can lawfully steal from the people without breaching the letter of the law (while driving a coach and horses through its meaning).

The development of cheque accounts allowed bankers to recreate the counterfeiting previously achieved with banknotes. This became formally known as "fractional reserve banking," and was one of the causes of the 1929 crash. Nobel Prize-winning chemist and later economist Frederick Soddy, writing in the aftermath of the crash, explained (in the currency system of the day) how the theft was conducted[5]†:

> *"Before the [1914-18] War it was considered 'safe' for the banker to keep some £15 per £100 of cash against deposits. That is, for every £100 deposited £15 of cash sufficed for the small cash demands, most of the depositors' purchasing power being exercised by cheque. We may take this 15 per cent for purpose of illustration only. It is doubtful if as much has been necessary for a very long time.*
>
> *"Now the whole secret of the system is contained in the fact that when a bank creates a loan and lends £100 to a borrower, to do so it need only have £15 of its depositors' money, or whatever the 'safe' ratio may be.*
>
> *"Thus, dealing throughout with averages, against the original depositor of £100, £15 of legal tender must be kept in the till, leaving £85 available to be lent to a borrower. It is true this borrower might demand it in cash, but, on the average for him no less than for the original depositor, only 15 per cent of cash, or £12 15s. is necessary, leaving £72 5s. free to be lent to a second borrower. Of this 15 per cent, or £10 17s., again suffices to be retained, leaving £61 8s. available to be lent to a third borrower. So it goes on until each £100 of original cash becomes a total of £666 13s. 4d. Of this £100 are due to the depositor and £566 13s. 4d. is owing to the bank from the borrowers.*
>
> *"The borrowers have to deposit with the bank acceptable collateral securities, which, if they default, the bank can sell, or try to sell, to recoup itself. But such securities are usually not sold. The bank charges interest upon the fictitious loan. At the modest 5 per cent bank rate the interest on £566 13s. 4d. is £28 6s. 8d. per year, which is, it must be admitted, not a bad return on £100 which the original 'depositor' has not lent.*

---

† Soddy is using the imperial money units of the day, in which there were 12 pence (denoted by the letter 'd' for denarii) in a shilling and 20 shillings in the pound.

> *"If the truth were known it would probably be found that this estimate is altogether too modest. At least since, if not before, the War the figures suggest rather a 7 per cent 'safe' limit than 15 per cent. On this basis a client depositing £100 of cash in current account enables the bank to loan £1,330, which at 5 per cent brings in £66 10s. 9d. per annum."*

To explain the problem that this compounding societal debt creates, Soddy posed the riddle of the "vanishing money":

> *"It is necessary to remember that those who are accommodated with loans from the bank really need goods of one form or another. They do not pay interest charges on borrowed money to hoard it. They very quickly exchange the money with others for goods. Once this has happened all distinction between the two kinds of money— genuine money owned by owners and bank money created to lend—disappears...*
>
> *"Even if it could be shown that the banks have broken the letter of the law in creating money, as they have certainly driven a coach-and-four through its spirit and intention, it does not in the least affect the conclusion that, for all practical purposes, there is no difference between genuine money deposits and those created by loan. Each is a valid claim to the wealth of the community.*
>
> *"Thus one may be tempted to think, when one reads that, of the total amount of bank deposits, three-fourths or four-fifths have been created by loans, that only one-fourth or one-fifth is really money genuinely belonging to the depositors, and that the rest is borrowed from the bank and owed to the bank at the same time and by the same people. This is not so. The people who owe the money no longer have it; they have for the most part exchanged it for goods. True they are continuously repaying it, but, as continuously, the bank is granting new loans to take the place of those so repaid. Practically the whole of the deposits are genuine claims to money lawfully owned by the individual depositors, but the money they claim has no existence."*

In the aftermath of the crash and, especially after the horrors of the Second World War, new laws and regulation were put into place to prevent banks from abusing their ability to create debt-based currency in so reckless a manner. Nevertheless, even with these regulations in place, banks continued to create currency when they made loans. Regulation merely allowed central banks to place limits on the extent to which they could do so.

It is no accident that this one – all too brief – period in our history, corresponding to the unprecedented and never to be repeated oil-based boom between 1953 and 1973, was also the one time in modern history when the workers' share of wealth increased. A combination of hamstrung banks and more interventionist states allowed currency to be directed in ways which, in effect, directed the relative shares of the energy available to the economy more equitably.

It wasn't to last. Steve Keen has likened the economic theory which developed during the upswing of industrial civilisation as the economics of the Wild West. That is, when the Europeans began to colonise North America, they had access to the resources of an entire continent. Shortages were almost unknown because the moment all of the resources in one location peaked, people could just migrate westward to unlock more. Indeed, even when they reached the west coast, they could continue on first to the Philippines and Cuba, and eventually to such benighted places as Iraq, Afghanistan and Libya to ensure that they continued to access the resources they required.

Economic crises during this period of upswing tended to be monetary. When resources peaked, prices would rise. The cost of doing business and the cost of consumption would also rise. Profits would decrease and businesses would seek to cut wages in response. As the downward spiral gathered pace, banks would become risk-averse; no longer creating debt-based currency to loan to businesses. It is for this reason that economists like Keynes urged governments to step in as investors of last resort. The point in the cycle where banks are withdrawing currency from the economy is precisely the point when governments should step in to print and invest currency directly.

In the period following the Second World War it worked on a massive scale. Had it not been for the Marshall Aid programme and various additional US government-backed dollar loan facilities in the aftermath of war, Western Europe would have been plunged into a similar depression to the one that followed the First World War. Instead, the Western states, together with Japan, were able to rapidly rebuild their war-torn infrastructure and embark upon the switch from coal to oil which unleashed the 1953-73 expansion. When, however, the same trick was tried in response to the crises in the early 1970s, instead of another round of economic growth, the result was "stagflation" – the economy continued to stagnate even as prices rose at alarming rates.

Part of the explanation is due to the sleight of hand of US governments in the post-war years. Marshall Aid, after all, was not solely driven by altruism. Many in the US government were concerned that in the event that Europe were plunged into depression in 1945, communist parties would take over and Western Europe would follow Eastern Europe into the clutches of the Soviet Union. Nor did the fear of communism end with Europe. In the 1950s and 1960s various US administrations made the fatal mistake of viewing a series of Asian national liberation movements as being communist-inspired. Military intervention to prop up corrupt authoritarian regimes became self-fulfilling insofar as they drove these movements into the arms of China and the Soviet Union as the only alternative source of support against the massive American military. This was most obviously the case in Vietnam, where the Americans found themselves propping up French imperialism against a movement which, to begin with at least, sought only democratic self-government.

The price of America's Cold War against the Soviet Union and its hot war against the people of Vietnam, Laos and Cambodia was the international position of the US dollar itself. Under the terms of the 1944 Bretton Woods agreement, the USA – the only major state whose economy was intact – agreed to maintain the value of the dollar against gold – an ounce of gold would be set at $35 dollars. In this way, all of the other states within the dollar system could treat dollars as being as good as gold. To fight its wars, though, the USA printed far more dollars than it had gold to back them up. However, where any other state would have generated *internal* inflation when it printed too much currency, America effectively exported its inflation to other states which traded in dollars.

West Germany was the first to notice the con, and from 1969 began to demand that the USA settle its trade accounts in gold. France followed suit, so that for a little over a year destroyers were used to ferry gold from the USA to Europe. The consequence was that the inflation – and unemployment – which had previously been exported began to find its way back to the USA. With an election coming up in 1972, Nixon began the process of ending the gold standard; resulting in inflation and unemployment once again being exported to Europe.

So began a decade of seemingly unmitigated crises which saw the boom years well and truly scuppered. Unemployment and social unrest increased. Trade union militancy grew. Standards of living fell. Prices continued to rise remorselessly. Investors simply ceased investing. Meanwhile, none of the orthodox economic policy solutions worked any more.

Seldom considered by economists is the question of why currency printing in the late 1960s and early 1970s failed to produce the same result as it had done in the 1950s and early 1960s. Why hadn't states been able to play their role as investors of last resort?

One clue is to be found in the partially artificial oil shock in 1973. Although in part a political reprisal for US involvement in the Arab-Israeli War, the roots of the oil shock are to be found in 1970 when US oil production peaked. Prior to that point, the Texas Railroad Commission (TRC) cartel had controlled the global oil price; setting it at a price which discriminated against Middle Eastern and North African states whose extraction costs were higher. The cartel achieved this by regulating the global supply of US oil. If prices rose, the TRC could order an increase in production; if prices fell, they could order a cut. After 1970, the TRC could only cut production – something which would play into the hands of non-US producers who desired higher prices.

In part, the 1973 OPEC oil embargo was a signal to the western states that the days when they could take for granted a rising supply of cheap oil were at an end. A rising supply there would continue to be; but cheap no longer. Less obviously, 1973 marks the point when global oil extraction ceased growing exponentially – a major problem for currency creation in general and for debt-based currency creation in particular.

Currency printing worked in the aftermath of the Second World War because planet Earth was awash with resources just waiting for someone to exploit them. Only a handful of states were industrialised and just one – the USA – could reasonably be considered an oil-based economy. As industrial states switched from coal to oil, and as far more *industrialising* states joined the oil economy, currency printed by states or loaned into existence by banks would ultimately translate into more demand for oil; thereby opening up the huge oil deposits located between the Caspian-Caucasus region in the north through Persia in the centre and down to the Arabian Peninsula in the South.

The currency created to drive this growth required, however, that growth continue to be exponential. This is obvious enough in the case of the debt-based currency created by banks when they make loans, since loans come with compound interest attached. And so economic growth – and thus, ultimately energy growth – most rise exponentially too. Government currency printing is less obvious because sovereign governments have the power to print currency *without interest* attached. The point, though, is that they only do this on rare – and generally extreme – occasions. For the most part, governments sell bonds to select investors in exchange for future taxes raised on businesses and households within their jurisdiction. And since the bonds have interest attached, governments also require tax income – and thus the economy/energy – to grow exponentially too.

Once the energy available to the economy stopped growing exponentially, adding currency to the economy resulted in inflation even as economic growth stalled. The result was the worst of all worlds; employment fell, leaving large numbers unemployed even as prices – particularly of essentials like food, utilities and housing costs – spiralled upward. In these circumstances, investment stalled; removing the basis for future growth.

Because the crisis of the early 1970s was a supply-side problem, the economic theories of the day had no solution. Economists assumed – and continue to assume – that shortages in raw resources – including fuels – are resolved through a process of substitution. In theory, if there is a shortage of a resource, its price will rise. As it does, alternatives which were previously considered too expensive will begin to be used. As this happens, increased production, economies of scale and technological improvements will gradually lower the cost of the substitute. Thus, a *temporary* shortage of oil is not a problem.

But energy is not the same as other resources. Its true cost is not so much in the price paid to extract and convert fuels, but rather in the energy input which is required to obtain useful energy for the economy. In response to the oil shortages in the 1970s, there was widespread investment in extraction from oil fields which had been considered too expensive to produce – notably the Alaskan North Slope, the Gulf of Mexico and the North Sea. But no amount of technological improvement could bring the energy cost of extracting oil from these fields down to the earlier cost of land-based US oil. From the 1970s, the global economy would have to pay more for the oil it depended upon so that even though the *volume* of oil extracted continued to grow, its energy cost and its price never returned to the boom-creating level of the immediate post-war years.

Economists – and economic policy makers – do not regard energy as the essential precursor of economic activity that it really is. Instead, they regard it as no different to any other raw material consumed in the process of creating goods and services. Indeed, few contemporary economic models bother any more even to use resources as a separate input; lumping them – and land – in with capital, with labour as the only other category. With such a narrow view, it is entirely understandable that they misunderstood – and continue to misunderstand – the nature of the crisis they were living through; prescribing at best temporary treatments which only served to make the ensuing crisis even worse.

In the 1970s, the economic view that rose to prominence argued that government currency printing was the source of the crisis. In attempting to maintain full-employment, governments had picked winners and losers with no regard to the marketplace. Businesses which were well past their sell-by date were artificially bailed out; thereby stifling competition from new, technologically advanced and more efficient businesses. Growing inefficiency across the economy translated into higher prices to the end consumer. Meanwhile, government currency printing provided leverage to over-powerful trade unions, allowing them to drive up wages in response to rising prices. The ensuing wage-price spiral for unionised labour led to mass layoffs among millions outside unions or in weak unions. At the same time, returns to investors shrank beyond the point where further investment was worth it. The resulting stagflation would ultimately destroy economies unless governments changed course.

The proposed solution was for governments to get out of the way. Instead of printing currency, governments should leave investment to the private sector. In this way the cost of money – as expressed in the interest rate – would settle at its true value. Businesses and workers would have to compete fairly in these new conditions; with only the most efficient remaining in business. At the same time, capital controls would be removed; allowing investors to move capital to where it could generate the greatest returns – which often meant moving to an entirely different continent. The introduction of equalities legislation further undermined wages by bringing previously untapped reserves of labour into the workplace. Finally, credit controls were gradually removed so that debt could replace rising wages to maintain household consumption.

The result of this "monetarism" was a major recession which saw thousands of business failures and millions of job losses. Nevertheless, inflation was rapidly returned to single digits even if interest rates remained in double figures. And as new oil deposits began to come ashore, economies began to grow again; although never to the heights achieved between 1953 and 1973.

In the wake of the "Big Bang" financial deregulation in 1986, banks were able to utilise information and communications technology to counterfeit on a previously unimaginable scale. Under the earlier fractional reserve system, banks had an incentive to be conservative in their lending. While they stood to make a considerable return over the lifetime of a business loan or a mortgage, it might be ten or twenty years before the full return was realised. In the meantime, a business might fail or a worker might become sick, unemployed or might die; leaving the bank with a loss. Banks could calculate the percentage of loans that would go bad, but they could never know in advance which ones. It was, therefore, in the interest of bank managers to get to know the businesses and households that they might lend to. It was also in their interest – given the local nature of banking at the time – to ensure that local businesses remained profitable. Thus, banks acted as the servants of business rather than the other way around.

An old idea which *always* results in catastrophe to anyone foolish enough to use it changed the nature of banking in the 1980s. With computing becoming more powerful and more widely available, banks could do on a global scale what had only been possible on a small scale in the past. They engaged in a process called "securitisation."

Banks knew with some precision the *proportion* of loans which would fail, but not which ones. Suppose, for example, five percent of all of the loans they made would go bad. Under the old system, they had to take the hit – and add the cost of the bad loan to the fees and interest rates on all of the other loans. But suppose the banks could use computers to divide up *the income* from all of the loans and repackage it into a series of investment vehicles each of which would contain the same proportion of risks. For example, a bank might divide the income from 100 loans – which include the 5 percent that will fail – into 100 new vehicles containing one percent of the income from each of the 100 original loans. Each of these new "securitised investment vehicles" would have the same 5 percent risk priced in.

The beauty of this system for the banks is that it removed the need to be conservative in their lending practices. Whereas previously they had to wait decades for loans to be repaid, by selling the income from their loans to third party investors, the banks effectively made their money immediately. From the mid-1980s banks switched from being conservative to being profligate lenders because – they thought – they had removed the inherent risk of loaning currency to businesses and households which might go bust.

For ordinary consumers, the period was marked by the remorseless intrusion of banking into everyday life. In 1980, few ordinary workers in the UK had bank accounts. Many saved with building societies; which had been the main providers of mortgages. But for the most part, workers were paid in cash which they then used to pay bills and buy the goods and services they needed. The early 1980s witnessed a big push by the government and the banks for wages to be paid directly into bank accounts. This was sold on the grounds of security and convenience, but it marked the beginning of the gradual transition to a near cashless economy.

Initially, basic bank accounts could only be used to store and move cash. Cheque guarantee cards came later, followed by separate debit and credit cards. With the growth of the internet, online banking services also took off; again providing convenience to consumers and borrowers. The big advantage, however, accrued to the banks. Currency which only exists as bits within a bank computer is even easier to multiply than the vault cash which had to be held as a fractional reserve. To all intents and purposes, computerisation and securitisation removed the need to hold reserves entirely; freeing banks to make as many loans as they chose.

Two obvious consequences of this were the growth in junk mail landing on our doorsteps and the indecent haste with which building society managers bribed their members to vote for them to become banks. The former was because banks effectively had a licence to print currency every time they made a loan. The latter was because building society managers wanted to get their snouts into the trough. Banks whose names reflected their local character – Midlands, National Westminster, etc. – morphed into global behemoths that were rapidly to become "too big to fail" as they loaned ever more newly created currency to ever less credit-worthy sections of the population; inadvertently unleashing the debt-based boom of the 1990s and early 2000s in the process.

By the late 1990s, investors were beginning to get jittery about the safety of the investment vehicles being offered by the banks. Although the economy continued to grow and the income continued to accrue, bank lending had gone far beyond the triple-A rated borrowers which investors had been comfortable with. To assuage these fears, banks turned to the so-called "shadow banking" (i.e. unregulated) sector to provide insurance on their investment vehicles, so that were they to fail, investors would still be paid. This worked for a while. But by the early 2000s, investment was faltering once more. And so, to keep the ball rolling, the banks themselves set up offshore companies to buy some of their own investment vehicles in order to keep the price up; and since these could be traded, they would buy and sell them to and from other banks.

The system began to unravel after 2005 when rising inflation prompted central bankers to raise interest rates. While much of the establishment media attention was on so-called "sub-prime" mortgage holders who could not afford to repay their loans, few stopped to wonder why these people had been given loans in the first place. One answer was that the banks looked the other way; using intermediate mortgage brokers to arrange the loans without looking too hard at the credit ratings – or lack thereof – of the borrowers. Perhaps the most important reason, though, was that the western world was fast approaching "peak debt." The people with the highest credit ratings had already bought their homes and paid off their mortgages. Those with middle rankings had taken up the loan offers which had arrived on their doorsteps and were now repaying mortgages. If the banks could not extend lending even further, then the Ponzi scheme they had created would stop growing; and when a Ponzi scheme stops growing it collapses like a soufflé. Everyone with an interest in the system – including existing home owners – had a vested interest in extending mortgages to sub-prime borrowers because the alternative would have been a housing market crash. And so everyone turned a blind eye.

Interest rates, however, are similar to taxes; the higher they go, the less disposable income we get to keep. This is annoying for those at the top but it is devastating to those at the bottom. Sub-prime borrowers who had just about been able to manage their debts while maintaining a basic standard of living were suddenly plunged into deficit – there was not enough money left to meet essentials like food, utilities and transport. And so people began to default; posting their keys back to the bank and seeking cheaper accommodation elsewhere.

Theoretically, the houses that sub-prime borrowers were handing back or being evicted from were assets of the banks. The banks could sell them and recover the outstanding mortgage debt. But that only works when the housing market is growing and there are more potential buyers than there are properties to buy. Following the 2006 interest rate rises, the opposite became true. There were suddenly too many properties on the market and fewer potential buyers to purchase them. House prices fell sharply and the banks were left with "assets" which had become liabilities.

Without the income from mortgages coming in, the banks could not meet the terms of the securities they had sold to investors. As this problem grew, the banks turned to the insurances they had taken out in the shadow banking sector. But the insurance companies were only prepared for ordinary levels of bad debt. As the number of defaults grew, insurance funds ran out and insurance companies went bust. The banks were stuck with the bad debt they had issued and could no longer meet their own commitments to investors.

Worse was to come. Not only were the securitised investment vehicles rendered worthless, but it turned out that the banks had been buying this worthless paper off each other. There was no appetite to end up with even more junk investments, and so the banks stopped trading with one another. This was the famous "credit crunch" which threatened to spill over into the real economy.

When someone takes out a loan to purchase something from a company which banks with a different bank, the banks have to find a way to move the funds between each other. Although the volume of transactions is high, the distribution between banks is reasonably even. So for the most part the banks can just cancel the transactions owed to each other. What remains can be settled by transferring a special kind of currency called "central bank reserves" or "M0" between banks. This currency, though, must be backed by real assets. And in 2008, it turned out that most supposed assets were actually worthless. And if the banks stopped dealing with each other, the risk was that global electronic payment systems would fail and even cash would become unattainable. Routine borrowing would be impossible.

Governments and central banks had no choice but to intervene. This, however, was where the Big Lie came in. The banking CEOs told the central banks and government officials that they had a "liquidity crisis" (note the use of language to obscure the issue). So what is a liquidity crisis? Perhaps the easiest way to understand it is to imagine that you ask a friend to lend you £20 until you get paid at the end of the week. You have an outstanding debt which you cannot pay *immediately* but you have an "asset" – the work you have done for your employer – which will be converted into currency – i.e. made liquid – at a later date. In the same way, the banks were claiming that they had assets – the junk investment vehicles and the repossessed houses that nobody wanted – which they could sell at a later date, but they lacked cash immediately. The obvious solution – if they had been telling the truth – was for governments and central banks to arrange a package of bailouts to provide the additional funds – i.e. liquidity – to get the banking system working again. Indeed, to ensure that the public wouldn't know which banks were in trouble, *all* banks had to be given the same bailout package.

The truth was that the banks were *insolvent* in the same way that a company that had bought too much unwanted stock is insolvent. Insolvency, of course, is dealt with in an entirely different manner – shareholders and senior managers are the first to lose out and remaining assets are distributed to creditors. In this case, however, the banking system was too big to be left to fail. At far less cost to the state – and ultimately to the tax-paying public, governments could have nationalised the failed banks so as not to lose the networks of branches, ATMs and computer payment systems, and then used their power to print currency to recapitalise the banks with a view to ultimately re-privatising them. In the meantime, ordinary depositors could be protected using newly printed currency while those who had presided over the debacle – the shareholders and the senior managers – would be allowed to fail. That this was not done, and that governments have ended up paying far more in bailouts and quantitative easing than they would have done through nationalisation, is a measure of the power of financial interests in the modern world. While people around the world have suffered a decade of stagnation following the crash, the tiny minority whose wealth is generated in the banking and financial sector have enjoyed a decade of uninterrupted growth backed by central banks which have pledged to do all that they can for as long as they can to maintain the current wealth disparity... capitalism for the poor, socialism for the rich indeed!

(3): THE QUEST FOR GROWTH

The creation of currency *with interest attached* creates a conundrum. Imagine that you borrowed the first ever pound, dollar or euro into existence. That pound, dollar or euro would be in circulation, but somehow you would have to find the additional interest. Where might it come from? The government could, of course, simply print it into existence. Governments *can* do this, but in the modern world they never do. And so the only place the interest can come from is yet more borrowing.

The paradox here is that if every business and household were to attempt to pay off their outstanding debt at the same time, all of the currency which drives the economy would vanish long before the debt could be repaid. Thus, in monetary terms, the currency supply simply has to keep growing; and this means that households and businesses simply have to keep borrowing. Indeed, even a slowdown in the *rate of* borrowing is sufficient to cause a recession.

If currency was all that was required to maintain human life and to meet human wants, there is no reason why this couldn't continue forever. Each generation could simply borrow even more new currency into existence than the generation before. But currency is only *a claim* on wealth rather than wealth itself. Nobody – households or businesses – borrows currency just to look at it. Households borrow currency to spread the costs of large purchases like houses, cars and annual holidays. Businesses borrow currency to spread the cost of capital, such as new premises, machinery and equipment. It is here that the magical world of infinite currency meets the hard reality of limited resources on a finite planet.

In the real economy, the things that we buy and sell require a great deal more than currency. They require people and organisations networked into increasingly long and complex supply chains which, in the modern world, stretch around the planet. You may, for example, buy a smartphone from a local store. But the phones they sell were shipped from an assembly plant in China. That plant, in turn, received components from smaller manufacturers across the Asian continent. Those firms brought together raw materials from around the world –

copper from Chile, tantalum from Australia, palladium from Russia, oil from Saudi Arabia, gold from the USA, etc. The mines that extracted those minerals used heavy machinery and trucks made in factories in the USA and South Korea, which themselves required components made in small plants in Asia, which also depended upon mined minerals from around the planet.

To grow the amount of currency in the economy, we have to make this complex interwoven global economy grow accordingly if we are to supply the goods and services which people are borrowing currency into existence to pay for. If we fail to do this, we get *inflation* – too much currency chasing too few goods. This is *experienced* as rising prices. In reality it is a devaluation of the currency which impacts different parts of the population unequally. Those who get to spend the new currency into existence effectively steal a fraction *of the value* of the currency which already exists. In doing so, they enjoy the face value (as it were) of the new currency before any of its value has been inflated away. Since the poorest part of the population is not considered "credit worthy," they are always the losers as they never get to spend new (uninflated) currency but must always use the devalued currency already in circulation. It goes without saying that they are also the least able to adapt to rising prices. Those in the middle occasionally benefit when they take out loans; but unless their salaries can keep up, what they gain from borrowing they pay back in rising prices. Only those at the very top – particularly the owners and chief officers of the banks themselves – get to enjoy access to newly borrowed currency on a scale that more than compensates for the general rise in prices later on; and they are doubly compensated by collecting the interest on currency that was never theirs to lend to begin with.

(4): Wealth pumps

It is not unreasonable to say that the forcible transfer of wealth goes hand in hand with civilisation. In its earliest stages, human settlement – once it becomes large enough that it cannot survive on its land footprint alone – gives rise to bodies of armed men, the rise of warlords and the beginning of wealth inequality. It is notable that pre-civilisation human settlements tended to have buildings that were the same size whereas from the beginning of civilisation the biggest buildings were the granary and the adjacent building – the one occupied by the warlord.

Wealth transfer was simple enough to understand. Either hand over your stuff to the warlord or have your head removed! This went both for people living within the civilisation and for those on the outside who were unfortunate enough to have some commodity that the warlord desired.

Complexity gave rise to more codified arrangements in which taxes were levied and in which all concerned had both rights (but not always the means to enforce them) and duties. In the early Roman Empire, for example, the duty to provide military service to the emperor was rewarded with a grant of land on retirement – a grant whose value wore thin as the number of military campaigns grew. The feudal system which emerged across Europe further codified rights and responsibilities to the point where we now know that in relation to the state – on paper at least – medieval peasants fared better than contemporary workers. Although wealth was transferred via the duty to work the land of Landlord and Church, the number of days worked was less than most modern workers have to put in to pay their taxes. Moreover, the number of Holy Days – from which we derive the word "holiday" – when peasants were not required to work was greater than the number of holidays enjoyed by many modern workers.

For the most part, these older systems operated without the need for money. Wealth was simply transferred up the hierarchies of nobility and church in the form of labour and military services and goods produced. Only in the case of itinerant soldiers, sailors and merchants was money – and taxation – required; because without taxation money would be worthless.

In the money economy which emerged out of the ashes of the Black Death, coins become a token for and a claim upon wealth. Instead of transferring wealth via a duty – such as handing over a portion of the corn you have grown or the flour you have milled – labour, goods and services are exchanged for coins of equivalent value. This is done on the understanding that when the time comes, the coins can be exchanged for labour, goods and services of the original value. In any money system, however, those who issue the currency and those who get to spend it first have considerable advantages over those who only receive it after some of its value has been inflated away. As we have seen, this can be done by debasing coins or by issuing more banknotes than there is precious metal to back them up.

As industrialisation gathered place, new means of transferring wealth were developed. As Marx observed, in a production-line system it was easy to hide the true worth of people's labour. By paying them only for the time they worked rather than a fair share of the value they helped to generate, employers and investors could transfer yet more wealth. In a similar manner, companies which devised internal currencies which could only be spent at the company store could price gouge a little more wealth by overcharging for the goods workers depended upon. This, though, is as nothing compared to the transfer of wealth that became possible with the modern, computerised banking system.

Politicians pedal the myth that government spending is paid for with taxes. That is, that income from taxes *must* come first. In reality, taxes come last. Current spending is paid for with government borrowing:

- The Treasury issues paper promises – called gilt edged securities in the UK or treasury bonds in the USA – to repay the amount borrowed with interest.
- Approved banks buy these bonds, which they sell to the central banks in exchange for special "base currency" or "central bank reserves" which are spirited into existence.
- The banks loan this currency back to the Treasury and the government uses them to pay for services, investments, pensions and benefits, etc.
- Once spent, this currency makes its way into our bank accounts where commercial banks use it as a reserve against which they loan out massive multiples of debt-based currency to borrowers. Theoretically, central banks set a reserve ratio which limits the amount of currency that banks can create. In practice since 2008, however, central banks have been prepared to underwrite *any* lending that the banks engage in.
- In the absence of an equivalent growth in the energy available to the economy, each additional unit of currency loaned into existence steals a fraction of the value of all of the currency already in existence so that inflation becomes endemic.
- To add insult to injury, ordinary people are obliged to sell their time, effort, skills and talents in exchange for this depreciating currency so that we *never* realise the value of the original work.
- To add further insult, the state takes a sizable part of our income in taxes with which it repays the currency which it borrowed to begin with.

- As a consequence, not only is the currency losing value with every passing second, but there is never enough currency in circulation to repay all of the debt – public and private – which has been created. If the government and the entire population paid back all of the currency it had borrowed into existence there would be just notes and coins – which account for less than one percent of all transactions – and a mountain of un-repayable interest.

The system is designed to transfer wealth from ordinary people at the bottom to the owners of the banks and to the recipients of corporate welfare who get to spend the new currency before its value has been inflated away.

This, however, is merely the *internal* wealth pump. There is an additional wealth pump upon which empires are built. All modern states have currencies. But some currencies are more valuable than others. Why should this be so?

When Britain emerged as the first industrial nation, it had already begun to build what would become the largest – by land area – empire the world will ever see. But industrialisation provided it with the means to grow its empire to an undreamed of size; making the homeland unimaginably wealthy in the process. This is because British companies manufactured goods and technologies which were highly desirable around the world. Steel manufactured in the valleys of South Wales, for example, made its way in ships built in Glasgow and Newcastle to form structures as diverse as the Sidney Harbour Bridge and the Argentinian railways. More exploitatively, having destroyed the indigenous cotton industry, the British forced the people of India to buy finished cotton goods from the mills of Lancashire. The point, though, was that it all had to be paid for in UK pounds.

Countries that wanted British goods, technologies or expertise had to obtain pounds either by selling their own produce or by borrowing on terms which inevitably favoured the British. This is how, for example, the British Army turned up as the "protectors" – not *colonisers* you understand – of Egypt. British and French banks loaned Egypt the funds to buy the technologies and skills to build the Suez Canal – which primarily benefited Britain and France by shortening the sea voyage to India and the Far East. When the Egyptian treasury ran out of pounds, the British Army moved into Cairo to protect the investment.

In the modern world an American empire constructed around a couple of thousand military bases around the planet has its hands on the pump. The wealth pump, though, operates in the same manner. An arrangement to protect the rulers of Saudi Arabia in exchange for a monopoly over the sale of oil effectively allowed America to stand on the jugular of the global economy. Countries which did not have oil or which had no means of refining it, had no choice but to obtain dollars. As with the British Empire, this inevitably meant borrowing or trading on terms which favoured America. And so, just as Britain had funnelled the world's wealth into London in the nineteenth century, America funnelled it into New York in the second half of the twentieth.

In this way, both within nations and across the world economy as a whole, the poor are made poorer so that the wealthy can continue to accumulate in a manner not dissimilar to the board game Monopoly. There comes a time, though, when one player holds so much of the available wealth that there is no longer any point continuing the game.

REFERENCES

[1] Eisenstein, C. 2011. *Sacred Economics: Money, Gift, and Society in the Age of Transition.* Evolver Editions.

[2] Keen, S. 2011. *Debunking Economics: Revised and Expanded Edition: The Naked Emperor Dethroned?* P6

[3] "Poll shows 85% of MPs don't know where money comes from." 27 October 2017. *Positive Money.* https://positivemoney.org/2017/10/mp-poll

[4] Watkins, T. 2015. *The Consciousness of Sheep.* P153

[5] Soddy, F. 1933. *Wealth and Debt: The solution of the economic* paradox. Omni Publications.

COMPLEXITY AND THE MYTH OF SUSTAINABILITY

The crisis of the 1970s which led us inexorably to the 2008 crash also served to raise awareness of the idea of "sustainability." At its simplest, the proponents of sustainability argued that we should give up our obsession with economic growth and, in effect, learn to live within our – or rather, Planet Earth's – limits. It is from this movement that we derive modern attempts to replace fossil fuel energy with so-called renewables including solar and wind power. It is also from here that we get our modern interest in organic and regenerative farming. Recycling has also grown as the best means of slowing the depletion of finite material resources.

There is, however, a fundamental flaw in the notion of sustainability. As sociologist Joseph Tainter points out[1], every collapsed human civilisation in the past ended its days desperately trying to *sustain* the way of life it had built. In so doing, energy-sapping complexity – more specialists engaging in even more discrete activities – was required to maintain the economy at the level it had reached. In effect, sustainability was even more expensive than unsustainable growth. The question is whether our global economy will be any different.

A large part of the problem is that while a majority of us might be in favour of the vague notion of "sustainable living," there is little agreement of what this means in practice. What one person or group thinks of as a bare necessity – such as a developed state's water and sanitation system – would be regarded as opulent luxury by the majority of the planet's population. For the best part of a century – and not without some success – the goal had been to raise the living standards of the majority. Living sustainably, in contrast, implies a levelling down in which the top ten percent living in the so-called "G7 states" would have to give up a large part of their living standards since, if everyone were to enjoy them, we would require more than one planet Earth to provide them.

Attempts at tightening standards of living even at the margins – such as the recent French government attempt to impose additional tax on diesel fuel – have resulted in political unrest and open rioting among those groups disproportionately impacted. In recent years, political parties such as the Australian and UK Labour Parties which have gone into elections with a "green" manifesto have been roundly defeated by opponents more or less wedded to yet more fossil fuel-based growth.

All too often in practice, sustainable living means getting *someone else* to lower their living standards.

Even if we could agree to take the hit, however, our efforts would likely be thwarted by the unforeseen consequences. The complex network of global supply chains which both keep us alive and provide us with the mountain of consumer goods that we could supposedly live without are only profitable at the margins. To give an important example, diesel fuel is the life blood of an industrial agriculture that maintains at least 3 billion *additional* humans today – without the massive agricultural machines which enabled a massive scaling up of grain production in the second half of the twentieth century, we would have struggled to avoid famine with a global population of more than 4 billion people. And yet here we are with close to 8 billion people on Earth today; with perhaps 10 billion expected in the second half of the twenty-first century.

The problem is that diesel fuel accounts for less than half of an average barrel of crude oil. By far the biggest fraction is petrol (gasoline) used primarily for private commuting. A small fraction goes to other essentials like the pesticides and insecticides which also allow nearly eight billion of us to be fed. The remainder finds its way into everything from plastic straws to toothbrushes and from paint to plasticine. These "waste" products effectively subsidise the diesel fuel that we depend upon, rendering it far cheaper than would be the case if that majority of a barrel of oil really was treated as waste and had to be disposed of.

Something similar happens with modern communications. The value of the internet – accessed by cheap computers and phones – as a store of human knowledge and information cannot be overstated. Unfortunately, the store of *useful* knowledge and information is all but drowned out by a barrage of inane noise ranging from videos about cats and pictures of people's dinners all the way through to ignorant political ramblings and the latest conspiracy theories. The point, however, is that for the useful fraction of the internet to be affordable – to both providers and consumers – *requires* that the cost – and advertising – is distributed across all users.

The same goes for all of the critical infrastructure that we depend upon. Transport networks only function because of the high volume of unnecessary goods being delivered. Public utilities are kept affordable by spreading the costs to all users; particularly those who can afford the higher price of profligacy.

For this reason, the idea that we could live sustainably by cutting out all of the apparently unnecessary things that we do is plain wrong. Attempting to do so would bring down the life support systems that keep billions of people alive. It is for this reason that an alternative USB model of sustainability has emerged in the mainstream. In this version nothing gets cut. Instead, those things which threaten to make our current way of life unsustainable are simply unplugged and replaced with a supposedly viable substitute. Plastic straws, for example, might be displaced by organic straws derived from fast growing plants such as hemp or bamboo; although it is not clear how many rainforests would have to be chopped to provide the land on which to grow these new industrial-scale crops. In the same way non-renewable technologies – like solar panels and wind turbines – which harness diffuse renewable energy can supposedly replace internal combustion engines and fossil fuel electricity generation.

Here, too, the knock-on impact serves only to make our life support systems unaffordable. Ironically, since solar panels and wind turbines depend upon fossil fuels at every stage of their manufacture, deployment, operation, maintenance and disposal, by displacing fossil fuels they ultimately render their own cost too high for the economy to bear (although this is currently disguised by lavish government subsidies).

What this points too is the probability that civilisation resembles a soufflé insofar as it is either growing or collapsing. There may be no "steady state" at which the global economy can be operated in perpetuity. This may explain the growing disparity between the policy pronouncements of governments of all stripes and the actions that they actually take. Even the greenest of them continues with – since 2008 – increasingly desperate attempts to maintain economic growth while mouthing the desire for sustainability.

It may be that we are doomed to continue on the treadmill of growth simply to prevent a catastrophic collapse. It may also be that collapse is built-in anyway simply because there is not enough left of planet Earth to be plundered to allow growth to continue for much longer.

This is not immediately obvious when viewed in geological terms. In almost every case, there are more resources beneath the ground than all of the resource already extracted by humans. The trick, however, is to find a (energy and monetary) cost-effective means of extracting these resources. There are, for example, more than enough minerals suspended in seawater to meet the dreams of every human on Earth. In a 2016 article for *Mining Weekly*, Keith Campbell reported that[2]:

> *"According to Stanford University, in the US, seawater contains 47 minerals and metals. Starting with the most abundant and proceeding to the least abundant, these are chloride, with a concentration of 18 980 parts per million (ppm) in seawater, sodium (10 561 ppm), magnesium (1 272 ppm), sulphur (884 ppm), calcium (400 ppm), potassium (380 ppm), bromine (65 ppm), inorganic carbon (28 ppm) and strontium (13 ppm). Then follow boron (4.6 ppm), silicon (4 ppm), organic carbon (3 ppm), aluminium (1.9 ppm), fluorine (1.4 ppm), nitrogen in the form of nitrate (0.7 ppm), organic nitrogen (0.2 ppm), rubidium (0.2 ppm), lithium (0.1 ppm), phosphorous in the form of phosphate (0.1 ppm), copper (0.09 ppm), barium (0.05 ppm), iodine (also 0.05 ppm), nitrogen in the form of nitrite (also 0.05 ppm) and nitrogen in the form of ammonia (once more 0.05 ppm). Thereafter, we have arsenic (0.024 ppm), iron (0.02 ppm), organic phosphorous (0.016 ppm), zinc (0.014 ppm), manganese (0.01 ppm), lead (0.005 ppm), selenium (0.004 ppm), tin (0.003 ppm), caesium (0.002 ppm), molybdenum (also 0.002 ppm) and uranium (0.0016 ppm). Then come gallium (0.0005 ppm), nickel (also 0.0005 ppm), thorium (also 0.0005 ppm), cerium (0.0004 ppm), vanadium (0.0003 ppm), lanthanum (also 0.0003 ppm), yttrium (also 0.0003 ppm), mercury (once more 0.0003 ppm), silver (also 0.0003 ppm), bismuth (0.0002 ppm), cobalt (0.0001 ppm) and, finally, gold (0.000008 ppm). Altogether, there are some 50 quadrillion tons (that is, 50 000 000 000 000 000 t) of minerals and metals dissolved in all the world's seas and oceans. To take just uranium, it is estimated that the world's oceans contain 4.5-billion tons of the energy metal... Knowing these minerals and metals are there is one thing; extracting them is quite another."*

Four of the most common of these minerals – sodium, potassium, calcium and magnesium – are commercially separated from seawater today. Campbell also suggests that as global demand for lithium – for use in batteries – grows, it may become commercially viable to separate this element from seawater too. However, in a paper in the journal *Sustainability*, Professor Ugo Bardi points to the limiting factor[3]:

"Traditionally, the most concentrated ions in seawater (e.g., minerals such as sodium chloride) were concentrated and extracted from seawater by evaporation. Ions such as Mg or K can subsequently be recovered by electrolytical processes. These methods are not practical for low concentration ions, for which the most general extraction method is to pump seawater through a membrane containing functional groups that selectively bind to the species of interest. No known membrane is 100% selective, but it is possible to create membranes that can retain a small number of species. The adsorbates can be extracted from the membrane by flushing it with appropriate chemicals, a process called "elution". After this stage, the metal ions can be separated and recovered by precipitation or electrodeposition.

"The scientific literature reports only two recent cases of experimental tests of extraction from the sea of ions other than the four most concentrated ones: lithium and uranium. None of these attempts led to the development of commercial processes.

"The problem with extracting minerals from seawater lies in the huge amounts of water that need to be processed."

The lower the concentration of a mineral in seawater, the more energy is required to process the water and to separate out the element. Common elements like salt, which humans have separated via evaporation since at least the Stone Age, are simple enough. Lithium and uranium are at or just beyond the energy limit after which the cost of the energy input is greater than the benefits provided by the element obtained at the end.

A similar process has been occurring with conventional mineral recovery. Centuries ago, miners could stumble upon nuggets of metals like gold, silver and copper, lying in the beds of streams where the water had washed away the surrounding rock. The Romans took this observation to its industrial conclusion during their occupation of Wales, where they used a series of aqueducts and pipes to raise the pressure of water to the point that it could blast away the side of mountains to reveal the seams of gold beneath. In the modern world we use explosives and diesel-powered heavy machinery to achieve a similar result; blasting the tops off mountains or drilling miles beneath the Earth's surface to gather massive quantities of mineral ores.

It is rare, though, to stumble across nuggets of pure metal today. Instead, overconsumption in the course of the twentieth century has forced us to seek ever poorer grades of ore from which to refine valuable metals. The problem is that the lower the ore grade, the higher the energy input required to separate out the metal. More rock has to be pulverised in order to smelt it; and each smelt produces less metal. It is for this reason that common metals such as iron, steel, aluminium and copper are often recycled; since the energy input is lower than processing low grade ores.

This energy input cost issue applies to energy itself. Most of the industrial processes that we depend upon in the modern world require heat and forces far greater than can be generated by harnessing wind or sunlight. Even after decades of deploying solar and windfarms, fossil fuels still account for 86 percent of global energy consumption – and even this relies on our taking coal-burning China's statistics at face value (something which atmospheric carbon dioxide concentrations argue against). The energy cost of extracting fossil fuels, however, has been rising inexorably.

The modern globalised world may be fantastically complex in comparison to the localised world of our hunting and gathering ancestors, but its dependence on external energy remains. In order to maintain the complex web of global supply chains which allow nearly eight billion humans to live on planet Earth, we must continue to obtain the external fuel that powers the economic system. In doing so, we take Adam's curse to ever deeper levels, since no sooner than we have secured a new energy source to support our way of life than the energy source itself begins to deplete. And as the energy cost of obtaining the energy source increases so all of our energy-dependent activities begin to suffer. Only a new and more energy-dense energy source can prevent us from some form of collapse back to a more primitive state.

To those economists, politicians and journalists trained to view the world in purely financial terms, the problem always appears as a shortage of money. How many of us, at some point in our lives, have uttered the words "if only I had the money I would..." But as we have seen, money – or rather currency (since it is not a store of value) – is merely a claim on the goods and services which will be available in the future. And since the production of these requires energy, the source of which is also depleting, creating ever more currency merely serves to devalue the stock of claims already in existence. Only if new currency can unlock a new low (energy) cost energy source or develop a new technology to harness energy more efficiently can the ratio of claims to actual goods and services in the future be reduced.

Since 1973 we have been subject to the effect of an increasing *energy cost of energy* which has resulted in a decreased flow of energy into the non-energy sectors of the economy. Initially, this was experienced as a productivity crisis because growth *slowed* to the point that increased prosperity could no longer be paid for by increased output. Offshoring production to areas of the world which had cheap labour and lax environmental and health and safety regulation allowed the restoration of prosperity for a shrinking minority in the developed states – although only at the cost of a ticking political time bomb caused by abandoning the ex-industrial working class. The continued strength of the petrodollar and associated currencies, together with the financial alchemy of the central and commercial banks, allowed a relatively brief period of rising debt-based prosperity in the late 1990s and early 2000s. But even this was predicated upon the belief that fossil fuel extraction would continue to grow; albeit at a much slower rate than had occurred between 1953 and 1973.

For the UK and the wider world, 2005 marked a sea-change. In that year, Britain – the world's first fossil fuel-powered state – became a net importer of all fossil fuels. No longer able to rely on the revenue from North Sea oil and gas, the UK faced an unpleasant economic future since, ultimately, oil and gas backed the modern GB pound in the same way as Sterling silver had done in the eighteenth century. The UK's problems were, however, eclipsed by the global oil industry reaching peak *conventional* oil extraction in the same year. The result was the chain of events which led to the financial crash of 2008, the ensuing depression and the growing economic and political crises which look set to bring down the entire global economy and possibly industrial civilisation itself.

As with every other extracted resource upon which our complex way of life has grown, there are more fossil fuels beneath the ground than we have ever extracted. As with those other resources, however, what remains is too expensive (in energy and monetary terms) to extract without withdrawing so much energy (and currency) from the wider non-energy sectors of the economy that the system collapses anyway. The choice before us is stark. Either we find new sources of oil, gas and coal – which, for environmental reasons, creates existential problems of its own – or we seek an alternative energy *powerful enough* to at least maintain the economy we have built. And if neither proves possible? Après ca, le deluge…

REFERENCES

[1] Tainter, J.A. 1990. *The Collapse of Complex Societies.* Cambridge University Press

[2] "Over 40 minerals and metals contained in seawater, their extraction likely to increase in the future" 1 April 2016. *Mining Weekly.* https://m.miningweekly.com/article/over-40-minerals-and-metals-contained-in-seawater-their-extraction-likely-to-increase-in-the-future-2016-04-01#

[3] "Extracting Minerals from Seawater: An Energy Analysis" 9 April 2010. *Sustainability 2010, 2, 980-992; doi:10.3390/su2040980.*

The Limits to Fossil Fuels

In 1865, a British coal industry economist, William Stanley Jevons wrote up a paradox which he had observed in the rapidly industrialising British economy of the nineteenth century[1]. At the start of the steam age, popular opinion held that soon steam-powered technologies would satisfy everybody's desires. At that point, demand for coal would begin to fall. Mines would close and miners would need to find alternative employment. Jevons, though, discovered that there was no limit to the uses that steam power could be put to so long as enough low-cost coal could be extracted. Instead of a slowdown in the use of coal, engineers kept finding new uses and consumers – businesses and households – kept demanding more. The Jevons Paradox, in effect, is that the more energy-efficient you become, the more energy you end up consuming.

At the time there was as much energy in the form of coal beneath the British Isles as there was energy in the form of oil beneath Saudi Arabia. Few people in the 1860s – the last decade when the British Empire out produced its competitors – were concerned about the possibility that Britain might run out of coal. At the time – and for decades ahead – there was more coal beneath the ground than all the coal extracted thus far. For all practical purposes to a nineteenth century mine owner, coal would last forever.

The Jevons Paradox, however, added a new dimension to this issue. The amount of coal beneath the ground was less of an issue than the requirement to constantly grow the volume of coal being extracted in order to keep up with commercial demand:

> *"To part in trade with the surplus yearly interest of the soil may be unalloyed gain, but to disperse so lavishly the cream of our mineral wealth is to be spend thrifts of our capital—to part with that which will never come back. And after all commerce is but a means to an end, the diffusion of civilization and wealth. To allow commerce to proceed until the source of civilization is weakened and overturned is like killing the goose to get the golden egg."*

If there are always more potential uses for a fuel than there is fuel being extracted at any time, then the entire system must continue to expand. If it doesn't, and demand outstrips supply, there will be damaging price increases which can trigger recessions and depressions. So long as there are new deposits to be opened up, this is only a short-term issue. The rise in price will result in new investment to open up the new deposits. As these arrive on the market, the price will stabilise once again.

By the end of the nineteenth century, a British Empire built on coal faced another problem identified by Jevons:

> *"Renewed reflection has convinced me that my main position is only too strong and true. It is simply that we cannot long progress as we are now doing. I give the usual scientific reasons for supposing that coal must confer mighty influence and advantages upon its rich possessor, and I show that we now use much more of this invaluable aid than all other countries put together. But it is impossible we should long maintain so singular a position; not only must we meet some limit within our own country, but we must witness the coal produce of other countries approximating to our own, and ultimately passing it."*

As an example of the problem, by 1900 Cardiff docks were regularly visited by Polish coal ships – no surprise there, since the coalfields of South Wales had long provided the power for industry. Except that the Polish coal ships were *bringing* coal from Silesia to power industry on the South Wales coast. That is, it had become cheaper to mine and transport Polish coal hundreds of miles to Cardiff than it was to mine and transport coal from mines just 25 miles to the north.

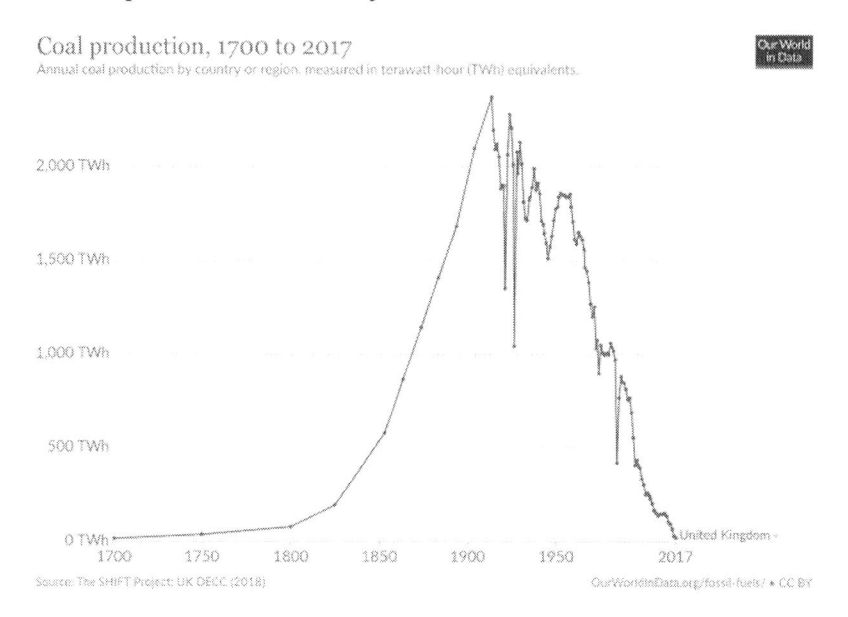

Coal production, 1700 to 2017
Annual coal production by country or region, measured in terawatt-hour (TWh) equivalents.

Source: The SHIFT Project; UK DECC (2018) — OurWorldInData.org/fossil-fuels/ • CC BY

War saved the British coal industry. The peak of British coal extraction came in 1913. From then on an increasing proportion of Britain's coal would have to be imported. The outbreak of war the following year, however, cut off the supply of coal from the Baltic. And because of its strategic importance as the power source of almost the entire war effort, coal had to continue to be extracted whatever the cost. It was only following the war that the consequences of peak coal had to be faced. The bitter industrial disputes of the inter-war years – including the General Strike of 1924 – centred around coal. With output declining, the mining industry had to cut its costs; and cutting the wage bill is always the easiest saving to be made. Because of its strategic importance, however, the mining unions always had leverage in the damage that a miners' strike could inflict upon the wider economy – a weapon that they continued to wield until their ultimate defeat in the strike of 1984-85 (the biggest industrial dispute in British history). At the same time, conflicted governments were torn between the need to protect a strategic industry and the ideological desire to leave the industry in private hands and to allow the market to arrive at optimum production, profit and wage levels. Again, an issue that was only resolved when, in the early 1980s, North Sea oil and gas had rendered British coal peripheral to the UK economy.

By the inter-war years, of course, oil – a new and more powerful fossil fuel – was beginning to replace coal as the key strategic resource. New, oil-based industries such as petrochemicals helped shift the balance of the British economy from the dark satanic mills of the north to the new hi-tech industries in the south. Today's "north-south divide" is a direct legacy of Britain's shift away from coal beginning in the inter-war years.

The fact that there was no more than a dribble of oil beneath the British Isles (the North Sea was inaccessible at the time) spelled the end of the British Empire one way or another. The decision to become unnecessarily involved in a Russo-German conflict in the Balkans in August 1914 merely accelerated the process. By the inter-war years the British Empire ruled over more than a quarter of the world's population but had access to only enough energy to preside over less than half as many.

Rather like British coal, the 1970 peak in US oil extraction was largely economic. The USA had access to so much oil from elsewhere in the world that it had no reason to extract more difficult domestic deposits. Indeed, the 1974 deal with Saudi Arabia which obliged oil producing states to buy and sell in US dollars removed the need to maintain the output growth of the domestic US oil industry.

The sting in the tale which Hubbert also pointed out was that the highest volume of oil discovery in the world came in 1964. It followed that the peak of global production would come in or around 2004. As it happened, the peak of global *conventional* oil extraction occurred in 2005; triggering the chain of events which led to the 2008 financial meltdown and the decade of stagnation which followed. But unlike the US peak or Britain's peak coal problem in the inter-war years, after 2005 there was no alternative source of *conventional* oil and no higher-density energy alternative fuel.

Between 2010 and 2018 US unconventional (i.e. energy-expensive) hydraulically fractured shale oil supplemented with Canadian and Venezuelan heavy (bitumen) oil has accounted for *all of* the growth in global oil extraction. Meanwhile almost all of the large conventional fields on Earth are already in decline. So that even though some states may have held on to some reserves against the day when US production falls once more, global oil extraction is now in permanent decline.

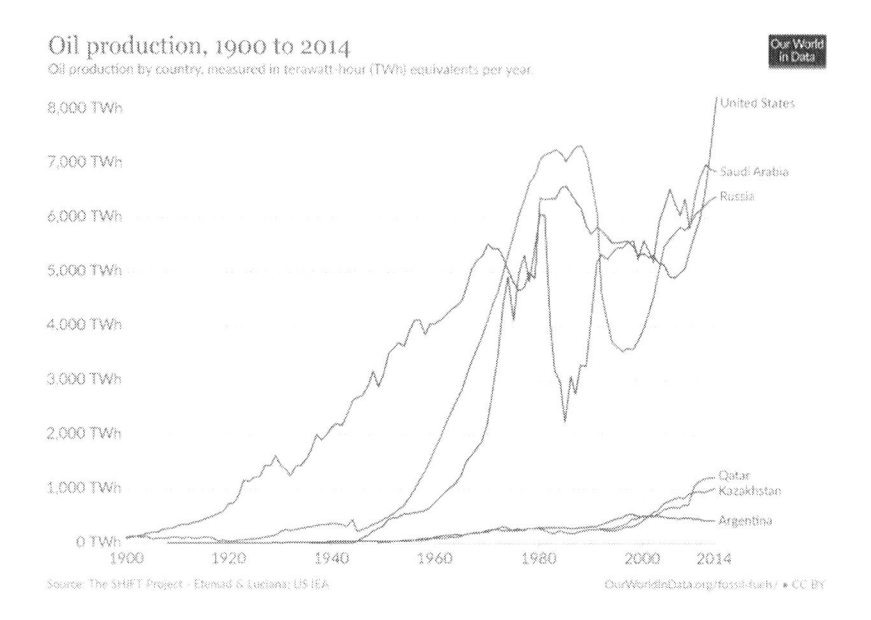

Oil production, 1900 to 2014

The US fracking industry was hailed as a technological miracle ushering in "a century of energy independence." In reality it was a monster created by Wall Street and the US Federal Reserve Bank. By forcing interest rates close to zero, they forced investors who needed higher returns to enter the "junk bond" market – unsafe investments where the risk of losing one's money is balanced with a far higher interest rate. Fracking was one of the high-risk industries which benefited; and for the ensuing decade companies spent billions of dollars extracting millions of dollars' worth of oil[2].

So long as the Federal Reserve keeps creating currency out of thin air, maintains low interest rates and convinces investors that they cannot lose, then the shale party will continue for as long as it takes to deplete the shale deposits. Unlike conventional oil fields, however, this can happen extremely quickly. The average hydraulically fractured well is 90 percent depleted in just three years; so that the fracking companies face a "Red Queen" syndrome in which they have to drill ever more wells just to keep the flow of oil growing. This allows them to sell just enough oil to *service* their debts. But when the flow of oil stops growing and investors ask for their money back, the party will come to an abrupt end.

The wider question is what happens to a civilisation that depends upon external energy for its life support when the most energy-dense fuel discovered to date begins to deplete?

REFERENCES

[1] Jevons, W.S. 1865. *The Coal Question; An Inquiry Concerning the Progress of the Nation, and the Probable Exhaustion of Our Coal-Mines*

[2] For a short summary of the economics of fracking, see: "The Fracking Ponzi gathers pace" 24 May 2016. *The Consciousness of Sheep*. https://consciousnessofsheep.co.uk/2016/05/24/the-fracking-ponzi-gathers-pace. For a detailed analysis see: McLean, B. 2018. *Saudi America: The Truth About Fracking and How It's Changing the World*.

Energy, Resources, Population and Consumption

For hundreds of thousands of years, the human population was made up of little more than a few thousand roaming bands across the entire planet. The first noticeable rise in population came with the Neolithic Revolution when, in a few river basins in favourable climatic regions around the world, the first settled agrarian civilisations emerged. Nevertheless, the total world population remained small as various civilisations rose and fell in their turn. It is only in the Middle Ages that the population begins to rise toward 500 million and only from the eighteenth century that the population begins to climb toward the first billion.

WORLD POPULATION (BILLIONS) 10000 BCE TO 2000 CE

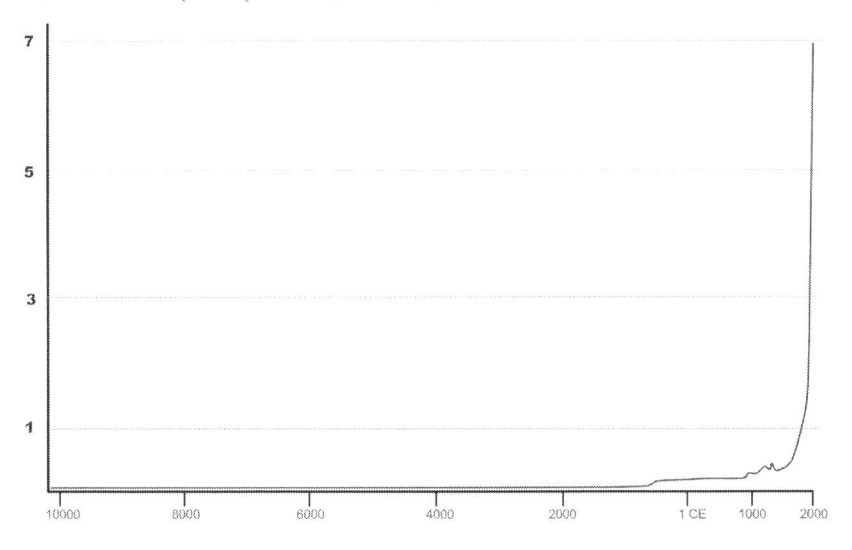

The uneven rise and fall of the population in the Middle Ages is due to the symbiotic relationship between humans and the natural Earth. Bountiful harvests in periods of benign climate allow the population to prosper and grow. During less benign periods, including "mini-Ice Ages," the result is hunger, disease and popular unrest. In this period, 500 million appears to be the upper limit of a human population living entirely on the outcome of annual solar energy.

From the eighteenth century, something begins to change. Having reached the first billion around the turn of the nineteenth century, things began to really accelerate. It took just 123 years (which included the Napoleonic, US Civil and First World Wars to reach two billion. A further 32 years (which included the Korean and Second World Wars) and the population had reached three billion. Just 15 years later and we had reached four billion; 13 years later, five billion; 12 years later, six billion; and another 12 years later seven billion.

WORLD POPULATION IN INCREMENTS OF 1 BILLION

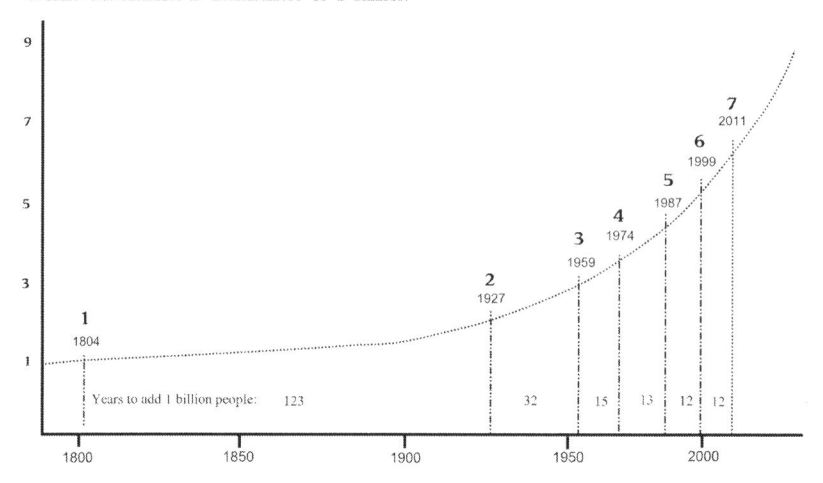

SOURCE: Population Division of the UN Department of Economic and Social Affairs

Why is it that a human population which seldom exceeded 100 million should accelerate upward so rapidly? The answer is to be seen in another, remarkably similar upward growth:

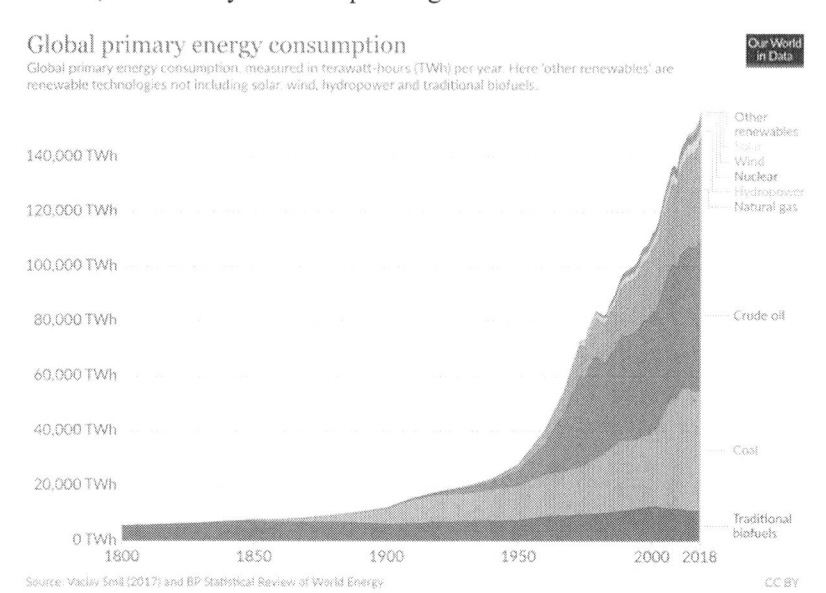

Prior to 1820 almost all of humanity had to subsist solely upon the solar energy arriving on Earth in a year. Most of the external energy we used came from food – and animals which ate food; from renewable energy – mainly wind and water power; and burning biofuels – mostly wood and charcoal. Gradually, though, we began to unlock a store of millions of years' worth of sunlight locked up in fossilised plants in the form of coal, oil and gas. As Frederick Soddy explained[1]:

> *"Still one point seemed lacking to account for the phenomenal outburst of activity that followed in the Western world the invention of the steam engine, for it could not be ascribed simply to the substitution of inanimate energy for animal labour. The ancients used the wind in navigation and drew upon water-power in rudimentary ways. The profound change that then occurred seemed to be rather due to the fact that, for the first time in history, men began to tap a large capital store of energy and ceased to be entirely dependent on the revenue of sunshine. All the requirements of pre-scientific men were met out of the solar energy of their own times. The food they ate, the clothes they wore, and the wood they burnt could be envisaged, as regards the energy content which gives them use-value, as stores of sunlight. But in burning coal one releases a store of sunshine that reached the earth millions of years ago."*

First coal, then later oil, provided humanity with the energy required to grow at the enormous rate witnessed in the past two hundred years. Indeed, the rate of growth – relatively slow between 1800 and 1930, but fast in the years after World War Two – relate to the particular fossil fuels which powered the economy. Coal provided a massive burst of energy compared to renewables, but as a lower-powered and solid fuel, its applications were far more limited than oil. Nevertheless, industrialisation was marked by a switch in population away from the land and into the cities; a process which was much more pronounced in the oil age than in the coal age. Indeed, one reason why so many Americans survived the Great Depression – and why many today will not – is that more than 25 percent of the US population in 1929 were directly employed in growing food. Today the figure is a little more than one percent (the UK picture is similar).

Fossil fuel-powered industrial agriculture, together with industrial petrochemicals – artificial fertiliser, pesticides and herbicides – allowed us to reach a population far in excess of anything Thomas Malthus – or even pre-Green Revolution horticulturists[†] – would have ever believed possible. Despite localised famines, we now grow more food per acre of land than at any time in history. And while doomsayers have predicted mass starvation for several decades now, it has yet to set in. On the other hand, global convenional oil extraction did not peak until 2005; and US fracking allowed global oil extraction to grow right up to 2018. We are only two years past the peak of oil production and to some degree renewables, nuclear, natural gas and – especially – coal (in Asia) may be able to take up some of the slack.

The problem before us, however, is that none of our existing energy sources are as powerful[*] or as versatile as oil. And so even if we are able to rapidly deploy wind turbines and solar panels or switch to natural gas or hydrogen as an alternative transport fuel, we are still left with insufficient energy to do all of the things we currently take for granted.

In 2020 we are well on the way to eight billion and are projected to reach ten billion by mid-century. Which raises the question, just how many humans can Planet Earth sustain?

The answer – unsurprisingly – is, it depends. If seven billion or so of us intend to live like the population of the USA at the turn of the century (things have gone down hill in the ensuing 20 years) we would need around five Earths to sustain us. If, on the other hand, we were prepared to live like the average person in Bangladesh, we would only need around a third of an Earth. To grow to ten billion, we could just about sustain ourselves if we adopt the living standard of the average person in Uganda.

This, of course, assumes that the volume of energy and resources available to us today will continue to grow. But as we have seen, as the energy cost of energy increases, so the energy available to the wider economy – including the energy required to exploit the resources

---

[†] Thomas Robert Malthus FRS was an English cleric, scholar and influential economist in the fields of political economy and demography. Malthus argued that population was limited by – by would often overshoot – the resources required to sustain it. The Green Revolution, or the Third Agricultural Revolution, was a set of research technology transfer initiatives occurring between 1950 and the late 1960s, that increased agricultural production worldwide, beginning most markedly in the late 1960s.

[*] Nuclear is *theoretically* more powerful but nobody has figured out how to utilise it at a scale and in a form where it might replace our dependence upon oil.

required – has to shrink. Worse still, because we have extracted resources like metal ores on a low-hanging fruit basis, we require *more* energy to extract the required resources.

There are also pollution limitations. There is only so much waste and heat that Planet Earth can absorb before planetary systems like climate, ocean currents and forest growth begin to shift away from the conditions which provide humans with a viable habitat. Raise the temperature high enough and we will be lucky if a few hundred roaming bands are all that is left of us.

The problem, however, is that few people in the developed regions of the world are prepared to accept the precipitous drop in consumption and living standards which would be required to make a population of more than eight billion humans sustainable. Nor are the much larger populations of the developing regions likely to voluntarily give up their recently rising prosperity. Only in the most deprived regions of Planet Earth would sustainable living seem like an improvement.

There is an old story about two young fish making their way down the river to the sea. Along the way they encounter an old fish on his way upstream to breed and die. As they swim by each other, the old fish says, "Hi boys, how's the water?" The young fish say hello and carry on their way. Some time later one of the young fish turns to the other and asks, "What's water?" We are just like this when it comes to the energy which surrounds us and is fundamental to everything we do. It has become so commonplace that we no longer notice it. And so, rather than understanding our current predicament as an energy crisis, different groups of people focus on different symptoms. This group focuses on global warming, that group protests the extinction of species, another group raises growing human exploitation and modern slavery, the group over there is concerned about resource depletion, and the handful in the corner are concerned with over-population.

A better way of viewing these symptoms is to see them as different dials on a single control panel. If the energy *available to us* falls, then we are faced with a trade off between resources – the building blocks of the economy; consumption – all of the goods and services; and population. One way this happens is if the primary energy which powers the control panel shrinks because more and more of it is needed to produce primary energy and to maintain the primary energy sector of the economy:

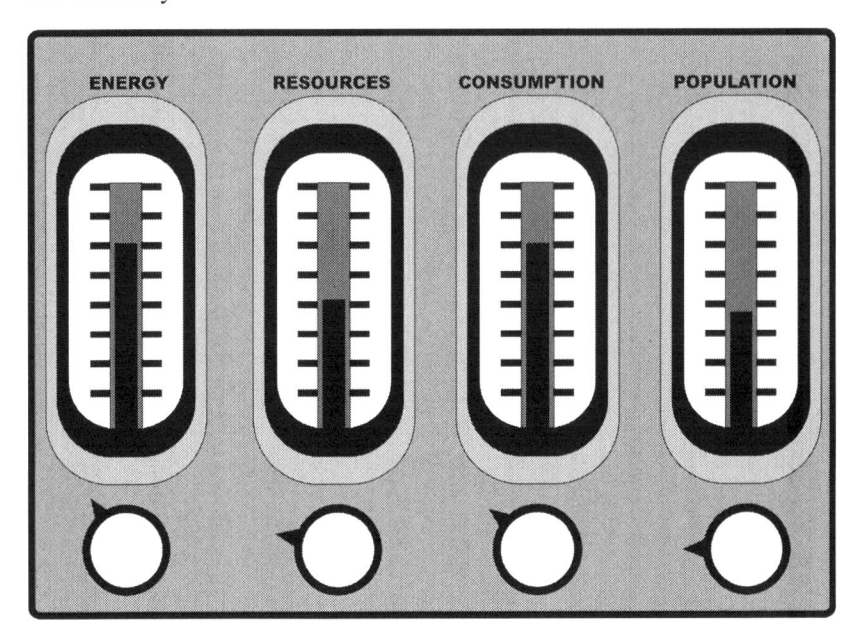

As the energy available to the wider, non-primary energy sector falls, we have to face a trade off between consumption and population. We can have a smaller population and more consumption or we can have less consumption and more people. This leads to the politics of the haves versus the have-nots, which expresses itself globally between the developed regions, the developing regions and the "global south." Within nations it manifests along lines such as gender, sexuality, race, age, class and disability. And as we have seen with the collapse of the neoliberal consensus in recent years, it is an explosive mix which is unlikely to improve any time soon.

The underlying crisis, though, is with the rising energy cost of energy. If by some cosmic conjuring trick, we could spirit into existence a new energy source more powerful and more versatile even than oil, all of those symptoms of the crisis would disappear. There are more than enough resources in the Earth's crust and, indeed, in the solar system beyond, to provide wealth undreamed of even by the handful of global godzillionaires of today. The energy and resources could easily be put to use clearing up the pollution and reversing the process of global warming. Industrial agriculture could be taken to unimaginable new heights; so that no human need go hungry. Population and the wider economy could continue to increase. Hell, even the banking Ponzi scheme could continue for centuries into the future!

There is, though, no such magic energy source available to us today. Various *theorised* means of exploiting nuclear energy have such potential; but currently nobody knows how to exploit nuclear energy at the scale required to replace and overtake oil. Meanwhile, the best we can hope for from non-renewable renewable energy-harvesting technologies is that they *may* slow the rate at which the energy available to us is falling. And if we are powerless to prevent that energy gauge on the left of the console from falling, then one way or another we will be forced to watch the other three gauges fall as a consequence.

REFERENCE

[1] Soddy, F. 1933. *Wealth and Debt: The solution of the economic paradox.*

WHERE NEXT?

Several future energy scenarios have been proposed; each in its way little more than wishful thinking at the time of writing. The three *broad* visions of the future are:

- Renewable electrification
- A hydrogen economy
- Nuclear power too cheap to meter.

Of these, so-called renewable energy is the easiest to debunk. To begin with, we need to separate what are – to all intents and purposes – infinite energy sources (sunlight, wind, water, waves, tides and geothermal) form the all-too-finite technologies designed to harness them. Wind and sunlight may be renewable, wind turbines and solar panels are most certainly not. Worse still, it is currently impossible to manufacture either without burning fossil fuels. Transporting and deploying them, of course, depends upon vast volumes of diesel to power ships, trucks and cranes. As an example of the fossil fuel use involved, consider this back-of-an-envelope calculation for a single windfarm in New South Wales[1]:

> *"The 65m long (2/3 the length of a football field) blades were individually trucked 530km from Port Adelaide in South Australia to Silverton, NSW, near Broken Hill.... that's three trips adding up to nearly 1600km or a thousand miles for you American readers.... and I bet they weren't cruising at normal highway speed either, almost certainly worsening fuel consumption. And I almost forgot the many pilot and escort vehicles per convoy.*
>
> *"Worse, a new road was built to bypass Broken Hill and avoid some roundabouts. now I realise the cost, both financial and environmental, of the road will be amortised over the total 58 turbines planned for this site, but all the same; it takes a lot of fossil fuels to build roads… especially that far from civilisation.*
>
> *"'There will be relatively constant deliveries from the start of the new year all the way through to about May.' states the ABC News website. If all the bits have to be trucked that far, three blades, a tower in at least two pieces, the nacelle (assuming it can be trucked in one piece), and god knows what else, I make it out to be almost 185,000km of truck miles, not counting getting cranes and reinforcing steel and concrete there. Oh and did I mention the trucks had to go back from where they came…? Make that 370,000km or*

more than nine times around the Earth… or almost the distance from the Earth to the Moon."

That's just the transport of the turbines. Add in the earth moving machinery, steel and concrete delivery and the cranes needed to erect the turbines and you might get to the Moon and back. That is just one tiny – 199MW – windfarm; and the 199MW refers to the *capacity* not the actual electricity generated. Remember that replacing the fossil fuels which even today make up 86 percent of global energy consumption requires that we deploy thousands of Terawatts of non-renewable renewable energy-harvesting technologies:

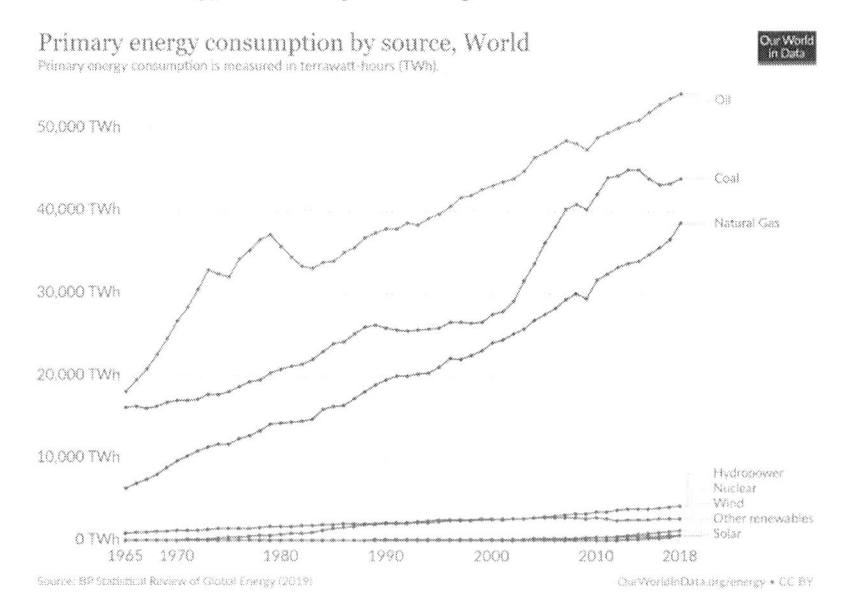

Primary energy consumption by source, World
Primary energy consumption is measured in terrawatt-hours (TWh).

Source: BP Statistical Review of Global Energy (2019)   OurWorldInData.org/energy • CC BY

It is worth noting, too, that hydroelectric power mostly installed decades ago accounts for the vast majority of the renewable energy we consume. Almost all of the planet's big rivers have already been dammed to generate power and there are few valleys left to be flooded. So a further large-scale expansion of low-carbon energy looks unlikely.

Renewable energy may cushion the blow as the global reserves of *accessible* fossil fuels deplete, but the idea that we can simply swap renewable energy for fossil fuel and continue growing in the way we did after World War Two simply lacks credibility.

Although absolute *quantity* is the main flaw in renewable energy, intermittency is often put forward as its main drawback. To resolve this *secondary* problem, many people look to the potential benefits of hydrogen as a fuel to replace oil. One reason for this is that unlike renewable energy, hydrogen at around 30,000 kcals per kg is considerably more energy-dense than oil.

Hydrogen – either for direct combustion or to power hydrogen fuel cells – has several additional advantages over the lithium ion storage proposed for renewable electricity. Since it can be stored under pressure as a liquid, it allows hydrogen-powered vehicles to be refuelled far more rapidly than an electric vehicle can be recharged. It also requires less new infrastructure – hydrogen tanks and pumps can be added to existing filling stations which already meet the various safety standards for explosive fuels. Finally – and far more persuasively – hydrogen fuel is much easier for governments to add fuel duty to since it is entirely separate from domestic electricity supply[†].

For all of its potential advantages, though, hydrogen comes with a long list of drawbacks. The most important of these is that although it is the most common element in the universe, hydrogen doesn't exist alone in nature. This means that to obtain hydrogen we must first use energy to separate hydrogen from the compounds that it commonly occurs in – most often natural gas and water. Almost all of the hydrogen currently used in industry – and by a growing fleet of hydrogen-powered vehicles – is separated out of natural gas in a process which vents carbon dioxide into the atmosphere. Outside school chemistry laboratories, few bother with the far more energy-expensive process of electrolysis to break water down into hydrogen and oxygen. This may change to some extent if the process is used to provide a storage solution for capturing excess wind and solar energy; as producing otherwise expensive hydrogen is better than paying the operator not to generate electricity.

Hydrogen storage is, however, a problem in its own right. Because it is the smallest atom in the universe, hydrogen can relatively quickly leak out of any container which it is stored in. This means that it can only be stored for a short period before use. Adding to the headaches, though, is the fact that hydrogen is extremely volatile. It is one thing for hydrogen to be leaking into the atmosphere from a storage facility;

[†] Adding fuel duty to electricity would mean asking non-car households to pay a proportion of the cost of recharging other people's vehicles.

it is an entirely different matter when hydrogen is leaking from a fuel tank into the interior of a vehicle where a single spark will be sufficient to kill everyone on board. These safety concerns are not insurmountable but they do mean that the cost of hydrogen power is going to be much higher than it might have appeared at first glance.

In terms of pure physics, breaking the bonds in the nucleus of an atom releases orders of magnitude more energy than breaking the electron bonds in fossil fuels has done. Nuclear weapons are evidence of this. However, humans have yet to figure out how to harness nuclear power. The pressurised water reactors that are currently used to generate electricity are so inefficient that more than 95 percent of their energy potential is wasted. As a result, they are less useful than gas-powered plants which use the same steam-powered turbines to generate the electricity. The need to pressurise water in order to produce super-heated steam means that nuclear power stations require active safety – if the operators simply walked away the system would overheat; causing the steam to separate into hydrogen and oxygen resulting in an explosion like the one at Fukushima in 2011. Less obviously, because the pressure vessel must be cast in one piece, and because each plant is unique, nuclear power has none of the economies of scale usually gained from mass production. The result is that construction costs and additional safety features render nuclear power uneconomical.

The UK government is currently experimenting with several alternatives. Small modular reactors which can be built and refuelled in a factory are expected to be the first to begin operating. The economies of scale suggested by the consortium behind them, if realised, would allow conventional nuclear power to compete favourably with wind and solar.

Three somewhat futuristic liquid-fuelled prototypes are also being developed; two using liquid metal (sodium and lead) and one using molten salt (fluoride). Because these are able to operate at far higher temperatures than conventional reactors, they do not need to operate at high-pressure (making them far less likely to explode). Moreover, because the fuel is dissolved in the liquid medium, almost all of it is consumed; leaving far less radioactive waste to be disposed of. Indeed, proponents of molten liquid reactors argue that they will be able to use existing nuclear waste as fuel (making them even more cost-effective).

The final UK alternative being developed is a nuclear *fusion* reactor which, if it could be made to sustain a continuous reaction, would provide enough energy to power several centuries of exponential growth. The downside is that nuclear fusion has been "twenty years away" for the best part of the last century; during which the best we have managed is to sustain a fusion reaction for just 101 seconds and at a cost of thousands of times more energy in than out.

Nuclear fusion is energy's Holy Grail, since – if we could figure out how to do it – we might have infinite, waste-free energy upon which we could develop technologies as magical to people today as our oil-based technologies would have been to a medieval peasant. As with all of these potential alternatives to fossil fuels, though, the hour is getting late. The energy cost of energy has already risen beyond the point where advanced western societies can be maintained. As a result we have a growing list of things that we understand how to do *intellectually*, but no longer have the available energy to do in practice.

Less obviously, there is a growing trend toward forms of simplification based on the need to *conserve* energy. Automated car washes – somewhat surprisingly[2] – have been largely superseded by hand washing other than in supermarkets, where they are offered as a loss-leader. Among the bestselling motorcycles in the world in 2019 was the retro-styled Royal Enfield 650 – a machine which bucks the trend toward ever more technology powered by ever larger engines. Fuel efficiency, it appears, is becoming far more important to bikers than the raw power desired by riders back when fuel was cheap. On a bigger scale, the same process has been happening in air travel, as airlines trade speed against fuel economy in order to prevent the cost of flying undermining profitability.

This points to an uncomfortable future for industrial civilisation. The proposed alternatives to fossil fuels either lack sufficient energy-density – solar, wind, wave and tide – or depend upon yet-to-be-invented technologies and materials to convert the raw *potential* energy into useful work. With the energy cost of fossil fuels rising dangerously and with the volumes extracted beginning to peak, we need a *rapid* transition to an alternative energy infrastructure if we are to maintain even a fraction of the standard of living we have become accustomed to. But energy transitions do not happen overnight.

Despite the first oil being drilled for industrial use in the 1860s, as a boy a little over a century later I watched working steam trains on our local branch line. I remember the winding gear in every village along the valley just a few miles north of where I grew up. I saw the coal tips that capped the hills on either side in the years before the 1966 Aberfan disaster (in which a coal tip collapsed engulfing the village and destroying the local school; killing 116 children and 28 adults). And I remember the grey-black film of coal dust which seemed to shroud everything. I remember the River Taff running black like treacle; full of suspended coal dust and the pollutant waste from heavy industry. It was only in the 1990s that the river cleared and the fish returned. That is how long it took the British economy to complete the shift from coal to oil. Only the deluded would imagine, even if some new energy technology were ready to be deployed tomorrow, that the economy could make the switch in months or years. Even if the most optimistic proponents of renewable, hydrogen or nuclear power were proved correct, it would take decades to make the switch from fossil fuels – decades that we no longer have... which poses the question, what ought we to do with the fossil fuels we have left?

REFERENCES

[1] "How sustainable is this…?" 7 December 2017. *Damn the Matrix*. https://damnthematrix.wordpress.com/2017/12/07/how-sustainable-is-this

[2] "An unlikely simplification" 9 April 2019. *The Consciousness of Sheep*. https://consciousnessofsheep.co.uk/2019/04/09/an-unlikely-simplification

A BROWN NEW DEAL?

In the early 2000s, as the installation of non-renewable renewable energy-harvesting technologies began to take off, analysts began to raise the threat of an "energy death spiral." In part, this concerned the way in which governments around the world were attempting to encourage the widespread installation of solar panels and wind turbines. In large part, though, it was the result of the rebalancing of available energy *away from* the non-energy sectors of the economy.

The basic problem with almost any new technology is that it requires mass adoption to bring prices down. To begin with, solar panels and wind turbines were far too expensive compared to electricity generation which had already been installed. Left to "market forces," power companies would have maintained their coal-fired power stations while expanding into the new and more energy efficient combined cycle gas turbine power stations. Wind turbines and solar panels were far too costly to install compared to the relatively small amount of electricity generated in return.

As an example of the difference, at the time of writing Orsted Energy's Hornsey One offshore windfarm in the North Sea is the largest windfarm on Earth. It cost £6bn to build and has an *installed capacity* of 1,200MW. For comparison, the nearby 840MW Keadby 2 CCGT power station is expected to cost just £350 million. This, note, is after decades of government subsidies designed to lower the cost of wind power. This, though, is just the beginning of the problem. "Installed capacity" is very different to "output." Whereas – so long as gas is still available – a CCGT station can operate continuously, the British Isles experience periodic low-wind high-pressure weather systems and high-wind low-pressure systems during which little or no wind generation can take place. During the most recent of these in January 2020, wind generation dropped to just 12 percent of UK electricity leaving the country dependent upon gas (50%) nuclear (14%) coal (8%) and assorted imports and small generators (16%)[1].

It is this kind of medium-term intermittency that the proponents of wind and solar power hope to iron out with some mix of energy storage. Although at present, pumped hydro is the only viable option and there are major limitations on the number of mountains which can be hollowed out to provide even a fraction of the storage capacity required. In any case, even widespread pumped hydro could not overcome the annual intermittency caused by differences in both supply and demand between summer and winter – obviously an issue with solar for countries as far north as the UK.

Even on a moment-by-moment scale, however, intermittency is an increasingly difficult problem to manage. In August 2019 the UK was plunged into a major country-wide power outage resulting from a power surge at the Hornsey offshore wind farm[2]. Systems at the offshore facility were set to disconnect from the grid in the event that a surge in output might damage the turbines. The sudden loss of power *ought* to have been balanced by a rapid increase in power (one of the benefits of CCGT) from the nearby Little Barford power station. Instead, the sudden demand for increased power tripped the Little Barford turbines, taking them off line too. All of this occurred in just seconds. Across the grid the result was a dangerous drop in frequency which, if allowed to continue, could have fried both Grid and customers' electronic equipment. Grid operators had no alternative but to disconnect millions of customers including, unfortunately, the national rail infrastructure operator; leaving thousands of commuters stranded in the Friday evening rush hour.

While there were things which could have been done to mitigate the problem, the crux of the issue is that as the penetration of renewable energy into the Grid passes 70 percent, as regularly occurs in the UK, constant Grid frequency – which prevents your computer, TV and refrigerator from frying – becomes increasingly difficult to maintain. When using a fossil fuel, Grid frequency is maintained by millions of tons of spinning steel turbines. Tiny temporary fluctuations in power output have no impact because of the inertia in the system. More importantly, the inertia provides vital time in which to switch to alternative generation in the event that a power station shuts down. Renewable energy generation lacks this inertia; and the more renewable energy in the system, the less inertia remains so that when a failure occurs there is no time to react.

This would be less of a problem if governments awarded contracts on the basis of "firm" (i.e. 24/7/365) electricity generation. This would oblige renewable electricity generators to provide – and account for – fossil fuel back-up until such time as reliable storage systems can be developed. The fact that this is not required means that renewable energy generators are essentially parasitic; relying upon but not paying the cost of fossil fuel generators which they are simultaneously putting out of business.

The practical consequence of this is that the additional cost of the switch to renewable energy generation is loaded onto consumers' bills. But this is a highly regressive means of paying because it leaves those who consume the least – mostly those at the bottom of the income distribution – paying disproportionately more for their electricity. This situation sets up a basic energy death spiral in which poorer consumers use ever less electricity in an attempt to keep their bills manageable. At the very bottom, people use pre-payment cards to – in effect – disconnect themselves when they run out of money. The loss of income to electricity supply companies – whose domestic supply is loss-making and subsidised by industrial and overseas income – means costs have to be met by raising prices. This, though, makes investment in rooftop solar and other forms of small scale renewable energy generation more attractive to those at the top of the income distribution; people who are often higher than average electricity consumers. The loss of that income further impacts domestic supply companies who must raise prices even further. And so it goes on with high-income consumers opting out, low-income consumers voluntarily disconnecting and the cost of the system landing on the shoulders of a shrinking group in the middle.

It is notable that in 2019 24 electricity supply companies went bust after promising customers prices that proved impossible to sustain; a 40 percent increase on the 17 which went into liquidation in 2018. This was due in large part to state fines issued on suppliers who don't source enough electricity from renewable sources; removing projected profit margins which unrealistically anticipated rising consumer demand.

The UK situation shows that there comes a point beyond which adding yet more renewable energy generation to the Grid creates more problems than it is worth. At this point, investment in storage, hydrogen and nuclear research and development together with drive to reduce demand would be more cost effective. Even so, so long as renewable energy generators enjoy all of the benefits while legacy fossil fuel and nuclear operators have to pick up the costs, there is a risk that the entire quasi-market in electricity generation will collapse into bankruptcy. The more this risk grows the more likely governments will be forced to insist that *all* generators provide firm electricity to the Grid. And if this fails, a return to the nationalised industries of the past may be the only option.

Oil faces a similar, but somewhat hidden, energy death spiral. This is because some oil products are worth significantly more to an industrial civilisation than others. Crucially, diesel is the life-blood of the economy as it is currently the only fuel which can power the heavy industrial machinery used in agriculture, mining, construction and maintenance. Without diesel, for example, we could have no windfarms or nuclear power stations. Diesel, however, makes up less than half of a barrel of conventional crude oil – and much less from a barrel of light shale oil. And so, in a sense, the sale and use of other products – primarily petrol (gasoline) – serve to keep the price of diesel to a minimum. The same goes to some extent for all of the plastic straws that people were getting worked-up about a couple of years ago.

Alternatives to oil products are far less developed than alternatives to coal-fired electricity generation. Nevertheless, without careful planning – which the current pandemic response has revealed that governments are not good at – there is a risk that diesel and the essential processes it powers might suffer a similar energy death spiral. For example, imagine that governments were so successful that they exceeded their target to replace internal combustion engine cars and light vehicles by 2050. As demand for petrol fell, oil refineries would be forced to invest in repurposing the refining process to produce less petrol and more diesel. This investment cost would have to be passed on to the end user; significantly raising the cost of fuel. As a result, the cost of every industrial and agricultural process which depends upon diesel would also increase, creating a general increase in prices across the economy. This, in turn, would result in consumers altering their spending patterns in a manner that created even less demand for non-essential (i.e. non diesel-powered) products and services. As a consequence the price of diesel would have to rise even further until the processes which depend upon diesel themselves became untenable.

In short, in an attempt to address one of the crises we face – man-made greenhouse gas emissions – we risk worsening a growing energy crunch as we run increasingly low on *affordable* fossil fuels. This is not to pretend that we can continue burning fossil fuels indefinitely. Climate change is real enough – though perhaps not the near-term extinction event which the more extreme climate campaigners claim – and fossil fuels are a finite resource which take millions of years to be created. One way or another we are going to end our addiction to fossil fuels. But if we are to give ourselves a fighting chance of avoiding mass starvation as oil-powered industrial agriculture is rendered incapable of supplying sufficient food for a population of more than 7.5bn humans, we need something more thoughtful than the simplistic "Green New Deal" offered up by parties of the political left. At the same time, if we are to avoid a similar mass famine resulting from whole tracts of farmland on planet Earth becoming barren, then we cannot bury our heads in the sand and continue burning fossil fuels in the manner proposed by the political right. If we are to have any chance of saving the best of industrial civilisation – or at least saving some of the more important aspects, such as a decent healthcare system and access to clean drinking water – we desperately need to give ourselves some room for manoeuvre. This is why I have tentatively talked about a "Brown New Deal[3]."

I am not personally hopeful that realistic, energy-dense alternatives to fossil fuels can be found in the time remaining to us. Nevertheless, governments and corporations around the world pump billions of pounds into research and development in this area, and some of the best scientific and engineering minds on the planet are working day and night on the problem. It would be arrogance and potentially hubris to dismiss the possibility of one or more of the proposed replacements for fossil fuels coming to fruition at some point in the next decade.

This said, humanity needs an urgent education in the physics and engineering of energy if we are to avoid being side-tracked into unworkable "green" energy scams which divert attention and funding from those areas where a potential solution may be found. In this, and despite the ad hominem criticisms, Michael Moore and Jeff Gibbs' documentary *Planet of the Humans* provides the kind of wake-up call that we need. Renewable energy generation will unquestionably have *a part* to play in our future energy mix. But it is no panacea. Like it or not, if we are to avoid the kind of economic collapse which will make the Great Depression look benign, we are going to have to settle for some mix of renewable energy, nuclear, hydroelectric and fossil fuels for the foreseeable future. And if we are honest, our collective behaviour demonstrates the truth of this. Environmentalists are no more inclined to give up their cars or the food and clothing flown in from the opposite side of the Earth than are conservative oil enthusiasts; and let's whisper the number of private jets that fly dignitaries and celebrities in and out of the annual climate change conferences.

Even if we accept that we are going to be burning fossil fuels for some time to come, the rising costs caused by supply shortages dictate that we are going to have to learn to use less energy in general. This is where the "New Deal" element *has to* come in. We have already seen what happens when the cost of switching our energy mix falls disproportionately on those at the bottom of the grossly unequal economies we have built since the financial deregulation of the mid-1980s. In France, an apparently modest additional duty on diesel fuel provoked the massive *gilets jaunes* (yellow vests) protests which morphed into a generalised uprising against inequality. Elsewhere, broad concern about falling living standards has played into the success of the nationalist-populist right; helping, among other things, to give us Brexit and the presidency of Donald Trump.

Once we acknowledge that value is neither the product of entrepreneurial capital nor an intrinsic property of labour, *then* perhaps we can talk seriously about how we ensure that nobody is left behind as we enter into an energy (and thus value) constrained future. If cuts in energy use are to be made, we must ensure the cuts fall on the broadest shoulders rather than leaving even more people shivering in the dark.

We need an urgent change in mind-set about fossil fuels too. For far too long we have treated them as an infinite resource that we consider less valuable than a glass of cola. This has led, for example, to a massive expansion of an ultimately unsustainable short- and medium-haul air industry when we would have been more sensible to have diverted the investment into expanding and electrifying local, national and continental railways. It has also created the extreme geographical distortions which have exacerbated a "north-south divide" which began to open up in the 1930s. Instead of encouraging the distribution of new industries and new employment across the country, it was allowed to become concentrated in big – and unsustainable – cities; driving up housing costs and obliging people to spend hours commuting as a consequence. Nowhere is this more obvious than in the UK.

While London has become the richest place in Northern Europe since the 1980s, nine out of the ten poorest places are in the UK's ex-industrial hinterland. For London's sake as much as for the rest of us, we need to rebalance this situation while there is still sufficient energy available to us to make the move. Throughout human history, large cities which could no longer be supplied by the hinterland beyond have rapidly

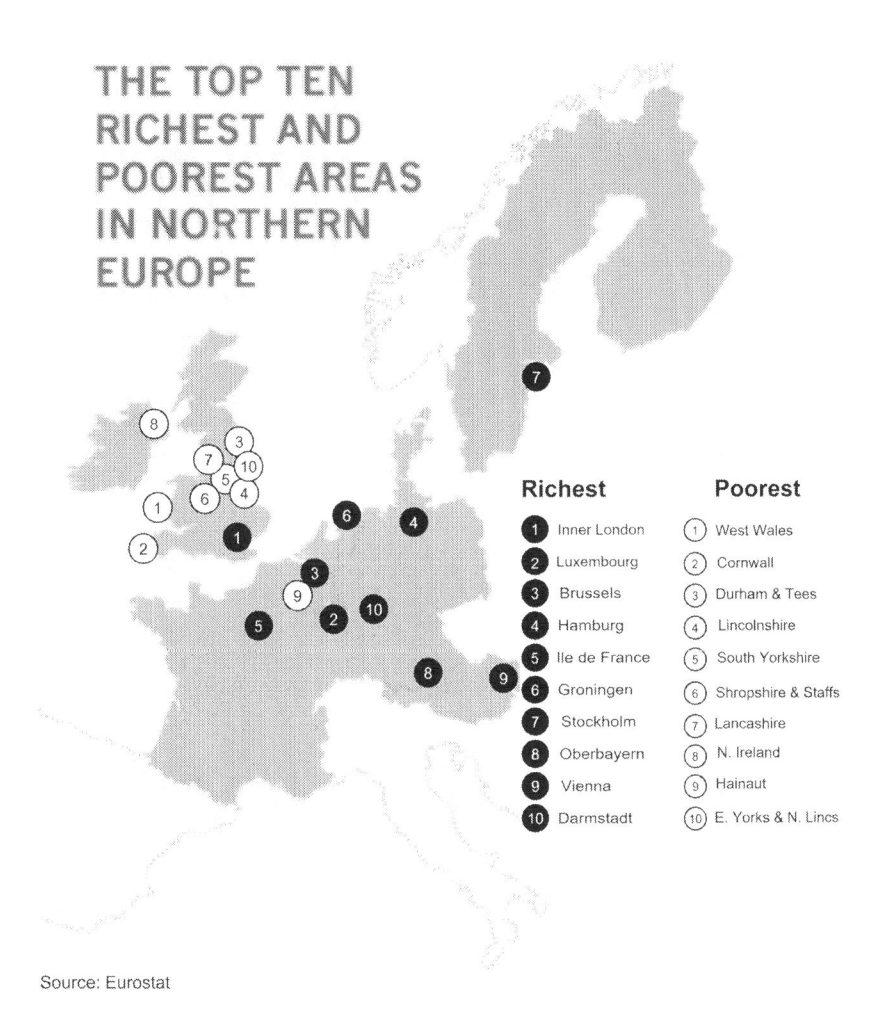

THE TOP TEN RICHEST AND POOREST AREAS IN NORTHERN EUROPE

Richest
1. Inner London
2. Luxembourg
3. Brussels
4. Hamburg
5. Ile de France
6. Groningen
7. Stockholm
8. Oberbayern
9. Vienna
10. Darmstadt

Poorest
1. West Wales
2. Cornwall
3. Durham & Tees
4. Lincolnshire
5. South Yorkshire
6. Shropshire & Staffs
7. Lancashire
8. N. Ireland
9. Hainaut
10. E. Yorks & N. Lincs

Source: Eurostat

crumbled to dust. There is no good reason to believe London – and similar cities – will be any different:

This is not just a question of curbing our fuel consumption. As supplies become constrained it is essential that the remaining supply of diesel is directed to those activities which cannot be powered any other way. For this reason, current plans to switch to electric cars and light vehicles – something that would also be more effective in a re-localised economy – should be preceded by a more immediate ban on diesel engines in such vehicles. Indeed, some kind of scrappage scheme could be employed both to boost the economy and to hasten the switch.

A worldwide process of re-localisation is essential, and will likely happen anyway. In an energy-constrained economy, shipping goods from one side of the planet to the other will become unaffordable. Thus, even though bringing manufacturing home implies higher prices, it may be the only way in which some goods can be supplied. And many items may, in any case, simply disappear. Trade will also need to become more regional than global. In an energy-constrained economy it will make little sense shipping – still less flying – goods across oceans when they can be sourced somewhere on the continent where they are needed.

Pull back the curtain and peer as far into the future as we can, and we might see a fork in the road ahead. One path involves some combination of the proposed alternatives to fossil fuels coming to fruition. If this happens, we may indeed get to keep the best elements of the civilisation we have built and to go on to create a new suite of post-oil technologies. And, no doubt, this path would also throw up global scale problems of its own for future generations to wrestle with in the same way that my generation had to come to terms with the prospect of nuclear war and the current generation has to come to terms with the threat of climate change.

The other path involves a prolonged period of de-growth in which the economy shrinks back to levels similar to the last time we had to exist solely upon renewable energy. This necessarily means almost everyone having to give up everything we take for granted about modern life. The few people who get to enjoy life in the big house upwind of the unwashed masses may enjoy some creature comforts, but life for everyone else is likely to be hard, short and brutish. And, of course, there will have to be far fewer of us. The last time Britain was self-sufficient in food we had a population of around 20 million. Today we have more than 68 million. The only way we get to make that transition in a hurry involves some manifestation of the Four Horsemen of the Apocalypse – Famine, Pestilence, War and Death. Given time, though, we might follow the course seen in post-Soviet Russia; fewer births and more people dying early and in a couple of generations the population is back to something more manageable.

A Brown New Deal aims not to choose which fork in the road we ultimately take. Nor does it offer some utopian magic wand in which we simply plug in the desired new technologies and continue with business as usual without missing a beat. Rather, it aims only to get us to that fork in the road – some ten to twenty years in the future – in a condition in which the next generation is best placed to take advantage of the choice before it. It is for this reason that I believe it would be foolish to prematurely cease using fossil fuels– as many green new dealers propose – and to pull out of research into hydrogen and nuclear in favour of non-renewable renewable energy-harvesting technologies that we know can only lock us onto the path to de-growth. Nor can we continue to follow the – as it were – black new deal on offer from the climate change-denying political right. Continuing to burn the remaining fossil fuels on business as usual would amount to a crime against humanity greater than any holocaust inflicted thus far. In addition to the devastation inflicted upon the environment, such an approach guarantees that when the fork in the road is reached, the only option will be the sudden uncontrollable collapse of industrial civilisation.

That collapse may happen anyway, of course. Nowhere is it written that humanity has to be eternal. And there are so many previous occasions when we humans demonstrably fucked it up that there is a very good chance that we really will bring about the extinction of our species. Nevertheless, we should not allow our children and grandchildren to go down without a fighting chance. So what is to be done?

The New Deal that gives humanity the best chance of reaching that future fork in the road intact is the one which involves creating new employment aimed at re-localising our economies in the most energy-efficient manner possible. This will involve the deployment of *some* renewable electricity generation but it will not be the cure-all proposed by the green new dealers. Indeed, creating employment within walking and cycling distance of people's homes will have a far greater impact on climate and energy use than any attempt to mass produce wind turbines, solar panels and electric cars in the quantities that would be required to maintain business as usual.

One way or another, the current fiat currency system will also have to end. We have already reached the point at which stock markets are the only place where investors can get a return; and only then because central banks are spiriting eye-watering volumes of currency into existence to prop them up. If the central banks were to cease this currency printing, the entire banking and financial system would collapse overnight. Outstanding debts would have to be written off. And so we need to pre-emptively write them off in a planned way – a modern version of the Biblical debt jubilees which had to be enforced every 49 years because the compound interest got out of hand. Instead of printing currency to prop up stock markets, we need the central banks to direct the currency to writing off outstanding debt. To make the process fair, the same amount of currency should be given to every adult as part of a new deal on the proviso that those who have debts must first pay off their debts while those who are debt free must spend – not save – the new currency.

In theory, nuclear energy - because breaking the bonds in the nucleus of an atom releases orders of magnitude more energy than breaking the electron bonds – could provide us with more than enough energy to overcome the problems facing us today. Moreover, several so-called "fourth generation" nuclear reactors which use molten salt and molten metal have already been demonstrated in laboratories. Indeed, in 2018 the UK government gave the go-ahead for seven prototypes to be built. Meanwhile governments around the world are looking to these as a viable alternative to coal. The jury is out on whether nuclear will emerge as a high-energy – and thus high-value – solution to our current predicament. I am personally not optimistic. However, some environmentalists at least believe that a new generation of nuclear technology can provide a solution to both reversing climate change and preserving the best elements of a modern industrial civilisation. For this reason, I believe that a brown new deal should include diverting research and development funding and key personnel into this area even at the expense of some of the more esoteric physics research currently planned – there is little point building machines that promise to explain the mysteries of the universe if we are likely to lack the energy to run them!

What of the rest of us? Most of us are destined to be little more than spectators as we make our way along the path to one or other of the potential futures ahead. We can participate in elections, write to our representatives and take part in demonstrations. But in six decades on this planet I have found these to be of little use; not least because much of the time the entire global economy runs on automatic pilot. It takes a national emergency to bring people together and to oblige governments to act. And offering up a credible course of action is far more likely to succeed than merely bemoaning the fact that governments didn't take action sooner.

What I do know is that the things which give meaning to life are seldom found in the material world. I am grateful, of course, to have lived in a time when a sizable minority of the human population got to live like gods. The ancient Greek Gods of Olympus limited their horizons to flying around the Aegean Islands. We, in contrast, think nothing of hoping on a plane and flying across oceans; often complaining about the lack of Wi-Fi along the way. I have bought foods in local supermarkets that the pre-industrial kings of England would have been lucky to taste just once in their lives. My nights have been illuminated by single light bulbs which give off more light than entire city districts used to enjoy in the days before electricity generation. Not once have I had to concern myself with the risk of viral or bacterial infection of my water supply. There have been many occasions when access to the routine medicine of the last six decades has saved me from disability, disfigurement or an early grave. If future generations are fortunate, they may yet enjoy lifestyles even more miraculous than this. But even if they are not so fortunate we, at least, should give thanks for having stood at the very apex of human achievement.

If we are to get the next generation to that fork in the road ahead in a fit state to make the right choice, we will need to learn to tread lightly on the Earth. We cannot continue consuming what remains of the resources available to us as if we are in a competition to exhaust our life support systems as quickly as possible. Nor can we continue to treat the people around us as if they do not matter. If we are to simplify, re-localise and harness the resources which remain to us in the best possible way for our children and grandchildren's needs, we are going to need to look out for one another along the way. We saw perhaps a glimpse of this in the early response to the Covid-19 pandemic, when far more people volunteered to help out than governments had planned for.

A brown new deal is not an easy option of the kind that governments can pay lip service to while continuing with business as usual and pretending the looming crises do not exist. It is something which will require support from across the political divide. And it will clearly fail to entirely satisfy anyone with preconceived ideas about the ease of energy transitions or that climate change and fossil fuel depletion is a hoax. For those who wish to give future generations the best chance of overcoming the crises on the road ahead, however, a brown new deal offers the least disruptive means of navigating the next decade or so.

REFERENCES

[1] "Today we're mostly cooking on gas" 20 January 2020. *The Consciousness of Sheep*. https://consciousnessofsheep.co.uk/2020/01/20/today-were-mostly-cooking-on-gas/

[2] "System failure" 2 October 2019. *The Consciousness of Sheep*. https://consciousnessofsheep.co.uk/2019/10/02/system-failure/

[3] "A brown new deal" 4 June 2020. *The Consciousness of Sheep*. https://consciousnessofsheep.co.uk/2020/06/04/a-brown-new-deal/

Also by Tim Watkins

The Consciousness of Sheep:
The Consciousness of Sheep provides a detailed and thoroughly researched explanation of the current predicament of Western civilisation; the ways in which the crises are likely to unfold; and the progressive responses that are beginning to emerge. It is a fascinating read for anyone interested in energy, economics, the environment, and the future of the human race. The message is stark but ultimately positive – it is time for us to develop a sustainable way of life for all of humanity.

Decline and fall: the Brexit years
On 23 June 2016 the British political landscape changed forever. Against the advice of the establishment, the British people had unexpectedly voted to leave the European Union; something than none of the political leaders had planned for. In *Decline and Fall: the Brexit years*, Tim Watkins sets out the long process of decline which provides the context in which the three years of political tragicomedy that followed the result should properly be seen; before presenting a compilation of three-years' of Brexit-related articles from his *Consciousness of Sheep* website.

The Root of all Evil: The problem of debt-based money:
When the Mafia make money they use the same plates, paper and ink as the government. The include the same security features and use the same serial numbers. Even to the most trained eyes this counterfeit currency is physically indistinguishable from the real thing. This being the case, why – exactly – is this Mafia money a crime? Who are its victims? Why should we care? The answers to these questions draw us into the fraud at the heart of our contemporary financial system; a fraud so vast in its scope yet so cleverly disguised that almost all of us treat it as normal while less than one in a million ever sees it. It is the fraud of debt-based money.

The Energy Theory of Value... and its consequences:
Karl Marx was 95 percent correct when he reasoned that one or more of the inputs into production must be paid far less than the value it generates in order to produce profit or "surplus value" at the end. Marx arrived at the blindingly obvious – and entirely wrong – conclusion that this input was labour. What Marx began to see toward the end of his life was that while labour could be exploited, automation meant that

something else must be generating surplus value… That "something else" turns out to be *Energy!*

BRITAIN'S COMING ENERGY CRISIS:

We dare not talk about this… Politicians dare not discuss it for fear of causing mass panic… North Sea oil and gas production peaked in 1999. The oil bonanza is over – the oil income spent. Britain is once again an energy importer. Worse still, we are increasingly dependent upon imports from the world's trouble spots and hostile regimes – Libya, Nigeria, several Gulf States and Russia. Even worse, successive governments have failed to invest in new electricity generation; let alone a switch from petroleum-powered vehicles…

AUSTERITY… WILL KILL THE ECONOMY:

The same message has been trotted out time and again by economists and politicians from all parties: "We must pay off the deb,t" "We have to balance the books," "We should have fixed the roof when the sun was shining," "Only by cutting public spending can we hope to return to economic growth." What if they are wrong? What if austerity causes recession? The early cuts triggered a recession, and economic growth has been anaemic ever since. What if these are the direct consequence of a misguided policy of austerity?

About the Author

Tim Watkins is the author of the *Consciousness of Sheep* website and the 2015 book of the same name, which addresses the unfolding environmental, energy and resource depletion, and economic crises that threaten the collapse of industrial civilisation; and possibly the extinction of the entire human race.

He graduated from University of Wales College Cardiff with a First Class economic science degree in 1990.

Between 1990 and 1997 he worked as a policy researcher with the Welsh Consumer Council where he wrote and published several key policy reports including: *Quality of Life and Quality of Service* – an investigation into the provision of residential care homes for older people - and *In Deep Water* – an investigation into the many problems that followed the North Wales (Towyn) floods of February 1990.

Between 1998 and 2010, Tim Watkins worked for the charity Depression Alliance Cymru, initially as a development worker, and between 2003 and 2010 as its Director. During that time he produced several mental health publications for the charity. Between 2001 and 2010 Tim Watkins was appointed to sit on several Welsh Government advisory bodies including the Health and Wellbeing Council for Wales, the Burrows-Greenwell Review of Mental Health Services in Wales and the Expert Panel on Depression.

Since 2010, Tim Watkins has authored a range of books relating to the "three E's" - Energy, Environment and the Economy. He has also produced a range of mental health and well being self-help books and booklets, together with two books on charity.

To find out more, please visit:
www.consciousnessofsheep.co.uk

You can also follow Tim Watkins on Facebook:
www.facebook.com/cosheep/

Printed in Great Britain
by Amazon